WHY DO
BOYS HAVE
NIPPLES?

WHY DO BOYS HAVE NIPPLES?

AND 73 OTHER WEIRD QUESTIONS THAT ONLY SCIENCE CAN ANSWER

With an introduction by Bobby Seagull

NewScientist

First published in Great Britain in 2019 by John Murray (Publishers)
First published in the United States of America in 2020
as *Where Do Astronauts Put Their Dirty Underwear?*
by Nicholas Brealey Publishing
Imprints of John Murray Press
An Hachette UK Company

1

Internal artwork by Jack Noel

A CIP catalogue record for this title is available from the British Library

UK Paperback ISBN 978-1-529-31749-7
UK eBook ISBN 978-1-529-31750-3
US Paperback ISBN 978-1-529-35249-8
US eBook ISBN 978-1-529-35915-2

Typeset in Avenir Light by Palimpsest Book Production Ltd, Falkirk, Stirlingshire

Printed and bound in Australia by McPhersons Printing Group

John Murray policy is to use papers that are natural, renewable
and recyclable products and made from wood grown in sustainable
forests. The logging and manufacturing processes are expected to
conform to the environmental regulations of the country of origin.

John Murray (Publishers)   Nicholas Brealey Publishing
Carmelite House   Hachette Book Group
50 Victoria Embankment   Market Place Center, 53 State Street,
London EC4Y 0DZ   Boston, MA 02109 USA

www.johnmurray.co.uk
www.nbuspublishing.com
www.newscientist.com

CONTENTS

CONTENTS

INTRODUCTION

Why it's important to ask 'why?'

AS MR SEAGULL the school maths teacher, I'm used to questions of a numerical nature being fired in my direction. And usually, I'm confident about being able to provide the answers.

However, if a student were to ask me something outside of my comfort zone, such as 'how do you design an alien?', or 'how can you measure the speed of light using a chocolate bar and a microwave?', or 'does wearing glasses actually make you cleverer?', I'd come a bit unstuck. I'm delighted that I now have this book I can refer my students to for . . . ahem . . . further reading.

As a child, what defined me rather than any innate intelligence was curiosity (no, I'm not referring to the 2012 NASA Mars rover called *Curiosity*, but my eager desire to learn about things). Curiosity might be responsible for killing the cat, but not a (Bobby) Seagull it appears.

Every Saturday, my Dad would take me and my brothers to our local library in East Ham, London. There was no objective apart from feeding our appetite to understand the world. Sprawled on the floor, I would sit there for hours with my brothers, devouring information on everything from the engineering marvels of the world to the wonders of how medicine works on our bodies.

Having an interest in science means that you're the kind of person who asks 'why?'. At one stage during my school days, my friends would call me 'why, Bobby, why' as a nickname, because I always wanted to understand more. If we saw a David Attenborough nature documentary on TV, I might ask a question like 'can that elephant jump?', or 'where are all the green mammals?', or 'why do tigers have stripes, not spots?'. I didn't always get an answer, but I kept asking questions.

So this is exactly the sort of book that childhood Bobby would have loved! If I had a *Back to the Future*-style DeLorean time machine, I would set the flux capacitor to the 1990s and put my foot on the accelerator to 88 mph so that I could give this book to mini Bobby (it would be totally worth the risk of causing a time paradox by meeting my younger self!).

When I'm teaching, I sometimes put key words or difficult bits on the whiteboard for my students to write down. Make sure you get your exercise book open for this.

The Science Council defines science as 'the pursuit

and application of knowledge and understanding of the natural and social world following a systematic methodology based on evidence'. Got that? It sounds very posh, but all it's really saying is that science is about getting as close to the real, objective truth as possible.

As a self-confessed number nut, I'm particularly excited that this book is called *Why Do Boys have Nipples? And 73 Other Weird Questions that Only Science Can Answer*. Why? Because 73 is a prime number (yes, you remember, a prime is a number that can only be divided by 1 and itself). And, like atoms in chemistry, prime numbers are the building blocks of mathematics.

But it gets even better. According to Sheldon from the TV show *The Big Bang Theory*, 73 is 'the best number'. This is because it is the twenty-first prime number. Its mirror, 37, is the twelfth, and its mirror, 21, is the product of multiplying 7 and 3. (Keeping up?) In binary, 73 is 1001001, which makes it a palindrome – a number that reads the same forwards and backwards. (See, maths can be fun!)

As a school teacher, I always tell my students what to expect in a lesson and it'll be no different for this book. Expect to be bamboozled by questions about the body and animals. Feast and be merry on the topics of food and drink. Look up to the stars for answers about earth and space. Best of all, perhaps, find out what grossology is! And if you still haven't exhausted your curiosity by then, get your hands dirty (but not too dirty!) by trying out some of the crazy experiments suggested here.

So enjoy tucking into this weird but wonderful book where science provides the answers to all those things you were wondering about, but were too shy to ask!

Bobby Seagull, 2019

About this book

THE WORLD IS full of baffling questions – and *New Scientist* is there to answer them. For over 20 years, readers have been submitting their everyday enigmas to the magazine's 'Last Word' column – with other readers writing in to answer them. All the questions in this book were originally asked there.

You can join in the fun too! Go to www.newscientist.com/lastword/ to see the most recent questions and answers, and email your own questions (and answers!) to lastword@newscientist.com. Or read the page '*Almost* The Last Word' at the back of the weekly magazine. Who knows, maybe your question or answer will one day feature in a book like this . . .

OUR
BODIES
AND
BRAINS

LIFE IS COMPLICATED, which means there's a lot going on in that brain and body of yours. In fact, your brain is in charge of most what you do, see, think and feel! Not bad for something that looks like a big wrinkly sponge. But it's not infallible – find out how you can trick your brain on page 11.

Have you ever wondered if wearing glasses can actually make you smarter? And why adults don't enjoy dizziness like children do? Are children's brains different to adults' brains, or are they just boring?

This chapter answers all these questions and more: why we pull funny faces when eating sour sweets, why a Pope drank the blood of three boys (hint: he wasn't a vampire), and why *do* boys have nipples?

Why don't adults enjoy dizziness like children do? Are they just boring or does something change in us as we age?

Love rollercoasters? Being spun around? Hanging upside-down? Feeling dizzy is pretty fun.

Kids obviously enjoy the feeling of dizziness – just look at how roundabouts in parks and playgrounds are packed. Children need stimulation to develop a healthy balance system, which is necessary to crawl, walk and keep our bodies upright, even on a rocking boat.

But what is our balance system?

Our balance system is controlled by three senses cooperating in complex harmony.

The first is our vestibular system – which is found in our inner ear. That informs us about the position of our head.

Our eyes are the second part. They tell us how our body is located in relation to the external world – so if we're standing still, jumping up and down or hanging upside-down.

The third are our proprioceptors and these are receptors in our muscles and joints that help us to figure out how our body is positioned in space (which is particularly helpful if we cannot see).

The thing is, all these elements mature at different rates.

The vestibular system is fully operational by the time we're six months old. Proprioceptors – the bits in our muscles and joints – need three or four years more. Surprisingly, the visual element takes the longest and isn't complete until we are about 16 years old!

The feeling of dizziness that happens when grown-ups spin around on a rollercoaster is similar to when you feel sick on long car journeys. We call this motion sickness. The reason this happens is that our brain is receiving conflicting information from the three different senses.

When our body is spinning on a merry-go-round or a rollercoaster, our vestibular system and proprioceptors can feel it, but our eyes can't work out what's going on because they can't see the horizon. Our brain is desperately trying to put a picture together, but because the main sense that we use for this is sight, it assumes that the other senses are hallucinating.

So what does our brain think?

Our brain assumes that we've been poisoned, and so it tries to get rid of the poison by making us throw up.

WHY DO BOYS HAVE NIPPLES?

HOW TO TRICK YOUR SENSE OF TOUCH

What do I need?

* three bowls large enough to put your hands in
* a decent depth of hand-hot water, tepid water and cold water chilled in the fridge
* your hands

What do I do?

Place one hand in the cold water and the other in the hot water at the same time. Hold them there for 90 seconds. Then place both at the same time into the bowl of tepid water.

What will I feel?

When your hands are in the different bowls of water, one feels cold, the other hot. Hardly surprising. But, when you place them in the tepid water they still feel different, even though they are both now in water of the same temperature. The hand that was originally in the hot water now feels cold, but the hand that was originally in the cold water feels warm. Weird, right? After both have been in the tepid water for a while they will both feel the same.

What's going on?

Human senses are relative, which means that they only measure the differences between things that we see, smell, taste, hear and touch. So, your cold hand feels that the tepid water is warmer and your hot hand feels the tepid water as colder. Your senses do not make absolute judgements on what is around them, only the relative differences of their environments.

But isn't this a bit unhelpful?

While this may lead to a few weird moments, it actually is helpful because it means we can focus on what is important and what is changing in the environment around us. It also means we can ignore things that are the same as they've always been.

This process has a fancy name: it's called adaptation.

Adaptation isn't just about touch. It affects all our senses and helps to prevent them suffering from sensory overload. Without it we would find the world exhausting because we'd literally be sensing everything *all the time*.

Adaptation is the reason we get used to smells and stop noticing them, or why our eyes become used to brightness or dark after we have been exposed to them for a little while. People who work in smelly places, such as refuse collecting or in fish-processing plants, are aware of the odour when they first arrive at work, but after a few minutes the impact is reduced as their sense of smell adapts to their surroundings. People who work in noisy environments are able to filter out the constant background noise — so you can tell that to your teacher next time he or she complains about the classroom being too noisy.

Does wearing glasses actually make you cleverer?

If you are a glasses-wearer, you might think you're going to develop phenomenal brainpower (reading this book will definitely help!). But surely that isn't really true . . .

Some very clever spectacle-wearers decided to find out. In an experiment in 1971, Michael Argyle and R. McHenry of the Institute of Experimental Psychology, Oxford, confirmed the fact that many believed that people who wear glasses are more intelligent than non-wearers.

How did they test it?

The two researchers made videotapes of performers both wearing and not wearing glasses. They presented them to the audience either as a static 15-second picture or as a video clip in which performers talked on a basic, non-intellectual topic – how they were going to spend their holidays – for five minutes.

Then the judges asked lots of questions about the spectacle-wearers. One of them was about IQ. They found out that the judges thought the people wearing glasses had an IQ that was 12 points higher, on average, than the non-wearers – which is a big difference.

So does it mean that people with glasses really are smarter?

Well, no. This IQ 'difference' only existed when the viewers looked at people wearing glasses in static photographs. Once the people wearing glasses opened their mouths and spoke in the videos, the magical effects disappeared. Wearing glasses doesn't make you smarter.

Why do we pull a funny face when we eat sour or bitter food?

I'm sure you avoid eating anything that will make you grimace. And so you should – your body wants you to.

Your body has lots of ways of reacting to nasty things like pungency and acidity. Sometimes these reactions will resemble involuntary defences, like you're being physically attacked by your nasty food! These reactions are similar in the animal kingdom, which means they are almost certainly primitive in origin (which means that our cave-dwelling ancestors did the exact same thing!).

If you ended up with a mouthful of a salty, bitter, acidic or otherwise vile and dangerous chemical (such as your own poo, for example) the natural reaction would be drawing down the corners of the mouth or gagging in preparation to vomit; salivating to clear your mouth and dilute harmful substances and puckering your lips to avoid letting anything more in. If those nasty chemicals were thrown at you, you'd close your eyes and throw your arms across your face.

But hopefully that will never happen, so what about less dangerous but still quite unpleasant things?

Foods like pickles or mustard make us grimace and shudder. Perhaps the reason these different levels of reaction have survived is because it warns other people about the unpleasantness of eating a particular food. It says: 'Bad stuff! Beware!'

Our cave-dwelling ancestors wouldn't have reacted with just a grimace when eating a hot chilli, they would gag and try to get it out of their mouth. The less vigorous signals of disgust evolved more recently than the primitive reactions, but they serve the same functions: warning of danger or nastiness.

When I'm in a car or on a train, why do things that were closer to us move faster than those further away?

You can try this one out when you're on the train or in a car on the motorway.

First, you'll see that objects further away look smaller. You can use your hands to show this: if you hold one hand close to your face and the other at arm's length, the one at arm's length will appear small, even though they are (probably) the same size.

Second, you'll notice that it takes more objects to fill the same amount of visual space if those objects are further away. For example, if the hand further away is half the apparent width of the one closer, it takes two hands to fill the same width.

Still with us?

Finally, think about something moving, such as your index finger traced slowly from one side of your palm to the other. If it moved at the same speed when it was further away, it travelled the same actual distance (a palm's width), but seemed to have travelled only half as far. So it would take twice as long for it to look like it had travelled the same distance. Distant things are not actually moving slower, they just look as if they are.

But sometimes it looks like things that are definitely still – like trees and houses – are moving. Why is that? Again you can test it for yourself.

Move your hand in front of your face. It's moving – no surprise there. Then hold your hand still but move your head from side to side. It still looks like it's moving, right?

Now for the science bit.

The answer is that the type of optical system that is used by our eyes causes us to see a particular object as 'smaller' the further away it is. This is called foreshortening.

Our field of vision is shaped like a cone, with the small end at our eye and the big end at the very limit of what you can see. Imagine standing at one end of a football pitch and looking towards the other end. Keep looking straight. At your end, you can only see the part of the pitch that is right in front of you. But you can see the whole width of the pitch at the other end. Now imagine your sister running from the left side of what you can see to the right side. If she is just in front of you it will take her just a few seconds to pass all the way across your field of vision. She is just covering a few metres, after all. But if she is at the other end of the pitch it will take her a lot longer to travel across the whole field of your vision – she'll have to cross the whole width of the pitch. So, she will seem to be going much slower because it takes her longer to cross what your eye can see.

How do traditional Inuit avoid scurvy?

Scurvy is a disease that is often associated with sailors – or pirates! – who couldn't get fresh fruit or meat to eat for long periods when they were at sea. You get scurvy when you don't eat enough foods containing vitamin C (which is found in foods like oranges, limes, berries and broccoli).

It's really nasty. People who have scurvy get spots on their skin, their teeth may loosen and fall out and they may bleed from the mouth, nose and gums. A person with scurvy will look pale and feel sad and they will not be able to move easily, because their joints hurt.

Humans – along with other primates, guinea pigs and fruit bats – cannot produce their own vitamin C and so need to get at least 10 milligrams per day from their diet to stay healthy. It can take several weeks or months before the body shows signs of scurvy. It starts with bleeding gums and, if left untreated, progresses to death.

So how do Inuit people, who live in freezing cold Arctic regions, make sure they get their orange juice?

The Inuit get all the vitamin C they need from their diet by eating raw meat. Muktuk – a mixture of frozen whale skin and blubber – is the richest source: 100 grams of muktuk yields 36 milligrams of vitamin C. This means that, weight-for-weight, it is as good as orange juice.

Raw caribou, kelp and more whale skin also provide more than enough vitamin C. Additionally, the Inuit people freeze any food that is not eaten raw, which helps to conserve vitamins, in contrast to cooking food, which destroys vitamins.

So no scurvy for them!

PALE? SAD? SPOTTY?

TRY MUKTUK

It's PACKED with Vitamin C!

WHALE SKIN

BLUBBER

We turn over up to 100 times during a night's sleep, so why don't we fall out of bed?

Some years ago, scientists at the University of Edinburgh investigated the reasons why big kids and grown-ups don't usually fall out of bed while asleep. But how do you find out what you get up to during your sleep? The scientists devised a simple experiment.

Volunteers slept on a very wide mattress in a warm room, with no bedcovers so that they would not be able to detect in their sleep where they were in the bed. Their head position was noted from a choice of four positions: nose to left, nose up, nose to right, or nose down. The apparatus used in the experiment wasn't complicated: it comprised a rugby scrum cap onto which the scientists stitched a circle of plastic tubing complete with a short piece of glass tubing. The tubing contained some mercury – the same stuff that's in a thermometer – and some needles that were pushed through the tubing wall at suitable points. The scientists then attached a dry battery so that small voltages were generated according to the head position. These voltages were recorded all night on a piece of equipment called an electroencephalographic recorder.

How did the scientists know when the volunteers were really asleep?

This was very simple. They arranged for a small sound to be made about every ten minutes during the night. If the volunteer was awake and heard it, they pressed a button attached to their clothing.

The scientists found that the sleepers turned at irregular intervals throughout their sleep, for example, nose to left, nose up, nose to right, then back again. But they never turned nose down. This meant that they did not roll over and over, so that they would fall out of bed. Actually, they remained in roughly the same position all night.

But what about small children? When do they stop falling out of bed?

You'll be pleased to know that the scientists didn't put their crazy sleeping cap on small children.

Instead, they watched younger children over a period of six hours while they slept. What they noticed was that during the night these little kids did turn nose down from time to time, meaning that they could turn over and over, and could have fallen out of their cots.

So what does it all mean?

It means that early in life we learn that it is difficult to breathe if we turn nose down when we sleep, and so we avoid it. As a result you can sleep safe in your bed tonight.

If were to put my brother in a sealed room, how much plant life would I need to keep him alive?

New Scientist definitely does not recommend that you try this one at home.

Okay, so you've locked your brother (or sister) in a sealed room, but you want to make sure they stay alive. How do you do it?

Well first of all you have to make sure that your brother has enough food and water. To stop this affecting the amount of oxygen too much, let's say you're going to feed your brother his dinner through an airtight hatch. Then he could eat all of his normal meals and the plants only need to provide his oxygen. You need more oxygen when you are using lots of energy, but if your brother spent all his time eating and dozing, he would need only about 350 litres of oxygen per day (the amount of oxygen in 1.7 cubic metres of air). This much oxygen is produced in full sunlight by typical vegetation covering a floor area of at least 5 square metres (a bit bigger than a king-size bed).

Now, some plants produce more carbon dioxide than others, but let's assume you're going to use the most productive 'C4 plants' such as sugar cane, then you could reduce the area needed to 2.5 square metres. Your brother would exhale 350 litres of carbon dioxide per day, which would enable the plants to grow 430 grams per day.

Got it? Now let's get more complicated . . .

If the windows in your brother's sealed room, plus artificial lights, supply 10 per cent of the amount of full sunlight plants would get outdoors (because glass stops some light getting through), you need to multiply the required area of greenery by a factor of ten. So the room indoors needs to be ten times as big as a garden space would be.

But we are assuming that the light is shining constantly. What if the lights go out at night? Well then you need to double the area.

Okay, got it. But what if you don't intend to feed your brother, but hope he will survive by eating the plants (let's hope he likes his greens!).

Remember that most bits of a plant are indigestible, so we'd need to double the area again to make sure that your brother doesn't go hungry. The inedible parts of the plants – plus your brother's poo – would need to be decomposed or burnt to carbon dioxide in order to recycle the carbon they contain. So, if your brother is well-trained, you'd need a plant-filled room that is about 100 square metres (10 metres by 10 metres) if using C4 plants, or 200 square metres (about 14 metres by 14 metres) if you are using other plants.

Why do boys have nipples?

Any ideas?

Maybe it's so that boys can check that their vests are on straight. Or they might be a useful summer holiday safety feature, warning us how far out from the beach we can safely swim . . .

However, there is a more sensible explanation.

Male and female human embryos are identical in the early stages of their development. Then, if the foetus received a Y chromosome from its father, a hormonal signal is produced and the baby turns into a boy (with the usual boy bits). If they don't get this signal, the baby stays female.

Yes, that's right, boys – you *all* used to be girls.

But what about nipples? Well, they had already

begun to develop when the 'switch to male' signal is received, so boys, you're stuck with them.

The Blood Cure

Good blood, bad blood, hot blood or cold. In the past, people believed that a person's character depended on the nature and quality of their blood.

Too grumpy? Blame it on blood. Too sad? Blame it on blood. Too lazy? You guessed it: blood.

So if someone was sick it should be possible to make them better by getting rid of some of the old blood and replacing it with something better, right?

To seventeenth-century doctors, there was nothing odd about this idea. In fact, this idea had been knocking around for centuries. Who you were, where you lived and what you ate determined the sort of blood you had – but it could change. Disease corrupted blood. Old age made it feeble.

Fresh young blood, on the other hand, had the power to rejuvenate. Pharaohs bathed in it to cure them of leprosy. Even Popes believed it had healing powers. In 1492, Pope Innocent VIII drank the blood of three boys, hoping that it would stop him from dying. (He died anyway – and so did the three boys.)

This silliness went on for centuries. Then, in 1628, an English doctor called William Harvey discovered that blood was pumped around the body by the heart. People stopped thinking that drinking or bathing in blood would have any effect and began to think about altering the blood itself.

In February 1665, a young Oxford doctor called
Richard Lower performed the first successful
blood transfusion – from one dog to another.
When he repeated his experiment before the
Royal Society a few weeks later, he caused
quite a stir. But he didn't stop with dogs. Lower
thought that the 'better' blood didn't need to
come from another human. He thought it could
just as well belong to an animal. He planned
trials to see if he was right . . .

The English weren't the only ones doing these
crazy experiments; the French were close
behind.

In June 1667, Jean-Baptiste Denis, a
mathematician, performed the first human
blood transfusion in Paris. The patient was a
15-year-old boy who was suffering from fever.

Dr Denis gave him a small amount of blood from a lamb. Like Lower, Denis wasn't worried about mixing blood from different species. In fact, he thought the blood of beasts was healthier because animals were not prone to overeating bad foods and drinking alcohol. When the blood was injected, the boy felt a searing heat along his arm, which we now know was a sign of an immune reaction to the foreign blood. But surprisingly, the boy actually got better.

So, a few days later, Denis tried the transfusion again with a healthy, middle-aged man. Like the boy, the middle-aged man felt a searing heat 'all the way to his armpit', but as soon as the experiment was finished he seemed fine.

But Lower, Denis and the other doctors had no idea of the risks they were taking. They didn't know any of the things modern doctors understand about blood clotting or immunology.

And they didn't know that the wrong sort of blood could prove fatal.

In December 1667, Jean-Baptiste Denis performed another transfusion. This time it wasn't because the patient was sick.

The patient was a servant called Antoine Mauroy. He had just got married but was behaving very badly, going out into the Paris brothels and often staying out for days on end. His wife was furious. She went to Dr Denis and asked if he could cure her husband of his 'madness'. Dr Denis thought a transfusion of blood from a calf, an animal with a suitably meek temperament, might do the trick.

The first transfusion went well and so Dr Denis repeated it a few days later. But the second time, Antoine Mauroy felt a violent pain in his arm and his kidneys. His heartbeat became irregular, and when he went to the toilet there was blood in his pee. But after a little while Antoine Mauroy got better.

And then he started behaving badly again. His wife insisted on another blood transfusion and this time, it killed him. Dr Denis was charged with murder.

However, the plot thickened because during the trial it turned out that Mauroy's wife had actually poisoned her husband. Dr Denis was released, but blood transfusions were banned in France and by the Royal Society in England before more bodies piled up. In medicine, it's a good idea to wait until medical science catches up.

ANIMALS

IF YOU WENT outside on a snowy day with no shoes on your feet would probably feel a bit cold, to say the least. They might even turn blue! So why don't polar bears' feet freeze when they walk around in sub-zero temperatures?

Animals do a lot of things that we do not: why do some birds stand on one leg for hours at a time? Why don't bats get dizzy when they hang upside-down? And why do dogs like jumping into cold ponds?

From orangutans and sloths to butterflies and elephants, this chapter is all about our furry (and not so furry) friends. Find out how you can fossilise your hamster, why tigers have stripes and why some scientists spend their time collecting whale snot and poo – yuck!

Is it true that elephants are the only animals with four legs that can't jump?

It is true that elephants cannot jump – from level ground anyway. In fact, as far as we know, even baby elephants can't jump.

But it turns out they are not alone. Probably all turtles cannot truly jump. It is also likely that some salamanders and large crocodiles, some chameleons and other lizards also cannot jump.

In fact, lots of animals can't jump. Hippos probably cannot jump and burrowing animals like moles, sloths, slow loris and other climbing specialists can't jump either.

Are we completely certain?

Well, no. The truth is that no researchers have done extensive research into animal jumping. We don't even know specifically why – in terms of detailed anatomical mechanisms and physics – any of these animals cannot jump. Some people say that it is because elephants have four knees (rather than two knees and two elbows) but this is a myth.

So what do we know?

What we do know is that large male African elephants weigh around 5 tonnes, which is about the same as 80 grown-ups. Asian elephants weigh only a little less. After elephants, the heaviest quadrupeds (animals with four legs) are the hippopotamus, which weighs about 3 tonnes, and the white and Indian rhinos, which weigh about 2 tonnes. Whether these and other large animals can jump depends on what you count as jumping . . .

Big jumps require strong leg bones and muscles. The feet have to exert a force on the ground equal to the animal's weight, so the bigger the animal, the stronger it needs to be to jump. In a big jump, the animal is off the ground for longer than it would be in a running stride, so its legs will be subject to larger forces at take-off and landing.

Physics tells us that if big animals were precisely scaled-up versions of smaller ones, they wouldn't be able to hold their own weight. This is because as something grows, its volume grows faster than its height does.

For example, if you have a square box with all its sides being 1 centimetre long, the area of one side is 1 square centimetre and it has a volume of 1 cubic centimetre. But a square box that is 3 centimetres long and 3 centimetres wide and 3 centimetes tall will have an area on one side of 9 square centimetres (3x3) and a volume of 27 cubic centimetres (3x3x3).

A similar thing happens with animals. As they get bigger, their weight would increase faster than the widths of their bones and muscles. An animal that is twice as tall and long as another would be eight times as heavy, but its legs would be only

four times as strong, and so less able
to jump.

Of course, even closely related animals of different
sizes are not exact scale models of each other. For
example, a 500-kilogram eland has relatively
thicker, straighter legs than a 5-kilogram dik-dik –
but the differences are not enough to let the
larger animals
jump as well as
the smaller
ones.

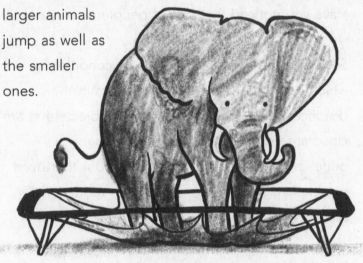

Other than size, a quadruped's anatomy or
physiology may be unsuitable for jumping. Some
desert lizards that burrow in loose sand have
greatly reduced limbs, tortoises have very slow

muscles and the limbs of moles are highly modified for digging. We have never seen any of those quadrupeds jump, and do not expect to.

Do any animals need to wear glasses?

Have you noticed that lots of people wear glasses?

Short-sightedness, or myopia, is a condition in which people struggle to see objects in the distance, which look blurred, while objects that are close are easier to see. There is probably a genetic factor in short-sightedness, but that does not explain why it is so common in modern society.

People who regularly focus their eyes over longer distances, such as sailors and mountaineers, are apparently less likely to become short-sighted. This might be because the muscles on either side of the eye can be trained to contract the eye, thus overcoming short-sightedness. Once a person starts wearing glasses, the need for such adjustment disappears – the glasses do the work for you.

But just because more than half of people wear glasses or contact lenses does not really mean that there's a malfunction in the entire human race. If you travel around the world, you will find numerous examples of keen sight that seem almost super-human to people from our side of the world.

So what about animals?

Primates brought up in captivity tend to become short-sighted. Myopia is caused when the distance from the very front of the eye to the back, known as the axial length, grows too long. So instead of focusing images on the light-sensitive tissue in the back of the eye, known as the retina, the lens at the front focuses the image in front of the retina, so it appears blurry. Changes in the power of the cornea at the front of the eye can also affect sight. Most change is likely to occur during the few years after birth while an animal is still growing, but may continue to a lesser extent for the next three decades in humans.

Better evidence comes from chicks, where a high degree of near- or long-sightedness can be induced by giving them contact lenses, and reversed, over a few weeks. There is a dramatic change at the back of the eye, which is accounted for by alterations in the rate of growth of the eye as the chick ages. Just like humans who squint to improve their vision, chicks can adjust the focus of their eye on an object, but this appears to exert little influence on growth.

Pets may show similar defects when they get beyond their life expectancy in the wild, and old dogs or cats often go blind from cataracts. Replacing a pet dog's lens is practically a routine operation nowadays. One need not give the dog glasses afterwards – just as long as it can see clearly enough to get at its food dish. It doesn't have to read the brand name on the tin.

Do whales and dolphins get thirsty? And if they do, how do they drink?

If you've ever swallowed a mouthful of water when swimming in the sea, you'll know that it doesn't taste good. But did you know that we humans cannot drink salt water to hydrate ourselves? This is because there is a lot of salt in seawater and in order to get rid of the salt you'd need to produce more urine than you'd had to drink, making you dehydrated.

Marine animals can't drink seawater either, so dolphins and whales do not drink.

So do they get thirsty?

Much of the water that dolphins and whales need comes from fish and squid, which can contain more than 80 per cent water. They can also obtain water through metabolising the fat in their prey, or breaking down their own blubber reserves, because that produces more water as a by-product.

In order to reduce their own water loss, they have similar internal designs to those of desert-dwelling mammals, including very complex kidneys that allow them to create incredibly concentrated urine, so they don't have to use as much water when they urinate out this waste.

As well as internal adaptations, marine mammals did away with sweat glands to stop any water loss through sweating. Instead, they use their surroundings to cool down.

How did dolphins' and whales' breathing holes evolve?

To breathe, whales use the blowhole on the top of their heads. Some whales have one blowhole, and others have two. When they reach the surface of the water, they use the blowhole to take in air.

How did whales end up breathing this way?

Blowholes are actually just nostrils that evolution has shortened and redirected towards the most convenient spot for snorkelling: the top of the head.

As in most swimming, air-breathing vertebrates – such as frogs, crocodiles, capybaras or hippos – whales' nasal openings are placed high up so they can breathe with as little raising of the head or snout as possible. They also have protective valves to keep water out.

However, most of the creatures in the above list are oriented largely towards the world above: they periodically leave the water in order to do things on the land, and they float with their nostrils and eyes just above the surface of the water, watching for food and threats. In contrast, whales spend all of their time in the water.

Scientists aren't sure exactly how whales ended up with their blowholes, but the answer might be found during the time of the dinosaurs . . .

Whales, dolphins and porpoises are all aquatic mammals known as 'cetaceans'. Their oldest relative is called *Pakicetus*, which lived about 53 million years ago. It looked a bit like a hyena with hooves and lived on the land. It had nostrils at the very end of its long snout.

About 20 million years later, we find the first 'true' whale. This was named *Basilosaurus* and it had nostrils all the way up its snout just in front of its eyes. *Basilosaurus* was fully aquatic, so this new position of its nostrils seems only sensible.

By 15 million years ago, the first modern whales and early dolphins all sported blowholes precisely where they are found on present-day species.

There's still one unsolved mystery, though.

Whales were not the first giants of the sea. Prehistoric sea monsters called 'ichthyosaurs' (their name means 'fish-lizard') were ancient reptilian predators that lived in the sea 20 million years before the dinosaurs walked the earth. They were particularly well developed for a marine lifestyle – with huge eyes, a jaw full of sharp teeth and a body that allowed them to swim super-fast – and they survived for 140 million years.

Yet even the very largest of ichthyosaurs had two conventional nostrils set just in front of their eyes, very similar to *Basilosaurus*. This meant that they had to lift most of their heads out of the water to breathe, which exposed them to attack by predators.

Ichthyosaurs became extinct 25 million years before dinosaurs were wiped from the planet, and scientists still don't know why. But the real question is, if whales and dolphins have evolved their beneficial breathing arrangement, why didn't the ichthyosaurs?

Why are orangutans orange?

In the forest being green helps animals to go unnoticed. Orangutans live in the rainforests of Borneo and Sumatra – which are also rather green – so why are they orange? Surely that makes them easy to spot?

But orangutans' colouring helps them blend in. The water in the peat-swamp forests where orangutans live tends to be a muddy orange. Sunlight reflected off this water can give the forest an orange cast, making orangutans surprisingly hard to see in dappled light. Many orangutan nests, up in the forest canopy, contain orangey-brown dead leaves, and some trees have reddish leaves, especially when young.

Ground-based predators would see orangutans in the canopy as a mere silhouette. In such circumstances, orange may stand out less than black, which may be more suited to blending in with the forest floor.

Dark African apes such as gorillas spend much more time on the ground than orangutans, while some other canopy-dwelling primates have a similar ruddy colour to orangutans. Among these are red langurs, which live in the same Borneo forests as orangutans.

If they live in the rainforest, why are they so hairy?

There are numerous possible reasons for this.

Orangutans are exposed to direct sunlight up in the canopy, so hair could serve to protect their skin from the sun.

It may also provide insulation and temperature control, trapping a layer of relatively cool air close to the skin by day and keeping the skin dry and warm at night and in cool, rainy weather.

Hair also protects against insect bites and helps break the outline of the animal's silhouette in the canopy when viewed from below.

Finally, dominant 'flanged' male orangutans have long hair on their arms and at the base of their back. This makes them look larger, helping them dominate other males and attract females.

How does the flounder change its colour to match the background? If you made a tiny blindfold for it, would the fish still be able to match its surroundings?

Did you know that it isn't just the chameleon that can change its colour?

Many animals change the shade of their skin, and some can even change it to a different colour completely. Cuttlefish have pigment-filled sacs that they can control with their muscles, producing colour changes and patterns that are really amazing.

A fish called a flounder isn't quite as good as the cuttlefish at changing colour, but it's still impressive.

The flounder belongs to a group that scientists call teleost fish. Lots of them, like the minnow, can change colour in response to their background. Light reaches their eyes from above and their brains compare it with what's reflected from the background below. The information is transmitted to the pigment cells in their skin via nerves that control pigment movement. Just like your school printer contains different ink cartridges, teleost skin contains pigment cells of different colours: melanophores (black), erythrophores (red), xanthophores (yellow) and iridiophores (iridescent). This allows the fish to blend in with what's below them – which is handy if something wants to eat them

Many flatfish, including flounder, go one step further than just reflecting what's around them. They develop skin patterns that make them even trickier to spot against the background.

So the flounder needs to be able to see what their surroundings look like. Blindfolding it would result in all parts of the system working to the same extent and the fish would adopt an intermediate dark or grey skin tone similar to that on a dark night.

And if the fish is receiving the same visual signals for a long time, the camouflaging effect will be longer lasting, hence the 'black' plaice

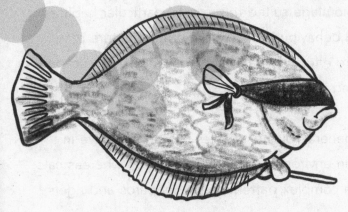

sometimes sold in the UK, which have come from the sea around the dark volcanic seabed off Iceland.

Why do tigers have stripes, not spots?

The beautiful striped markings on tigers' coats are unique in the cat family. Other closely related big cats have spotty rosette or cloud-shaped body markings (leopards, jaguars and clouded leopards) or plain coats (lions). Why is that?

Work by a team at the University of Bristol has shown that cat patterning evolved to provide camouflage suited to the cats' particular habitats and behaviours, enabling them to capture prey more effectively (and, for smaller cats, to escape being eaten themselves!).

In general, plainer species such as lions live in open environments and hunt by day, whereas cats with complex patterning like leopards and tigers have more nocturnal habits and live in environments with more trees.

Unfortunately, with no other striped cats around besides tigers, scientists cannot use the same methods to find out what drove tigers to depart from the ancestral big-cat pattern. Tigers are much bigger than jaguars and leopards, but in general they have a similar ecology, and tigers' historical range and habitat overlap considerably with those of leopards.

So why don't they look similar?

One idea is that compared with the typical leopard habitat, the average tiger habitat contains a lot of vertical features such as bamboo. Proving this would have once been straightforward except that with the tigers' range now so shrunken, it is hard to know exactly what sort of forest their coat evolved in. Tigers are obviously well camouflaged, yet the factors behind their appearance remain a mystery.

Here's an intriguing fact though: the team at the University of Bristol has discovered that the patterns of big-cat fur change relatively rapidly (over evolutionary timescales). So one day our descendants might wonder at the beauty of striped leopards and spotty tigers . . .

Why don't bats get dizzy when they hang upside-down?

When you think of bats, you usually think of them in one of two conditions: hanging upside-down resting, or flitting about pulling high-G turns in the dark. So why don't they get dizzy?

It is impossible to know for sure whether or not an animal is dizzy, because it can't tell you if it is. However, we can have a good guess at whether an animal is dizzy from how it behaves. For example, if an animal is aimlessly walking in circles, fumbling or falling over, then it is probably dizzy.

In the last chapter, we looked at what causes dizziness in human grown-ups: a conflict between what you are sensing in your inner ears and bodies, and what you are seeing. Like us, bats also have a balance mechanism, but theirs has evolved in a number of ways that allow them to hunt and hang without the problems that humans would face.

So what are they?

First, some bats have specialisations in the part of their inner ears that generates sensory signals for controlling balance. Their sacculus, which in humans acts as a gravity sensor to help us stand upright, is slightly rotated forwards. This enables it to tell the bat if its nose is pointing up or down, which is more useful in flight.

Second, their semicircular canals in the inner ear, which sense rotation of the head, have an internal structure more like a bird's than a human's. This probably allows them to make high-speed turns without the fluid in the canals sloshing back and forth too much.

Last, if you photograph bats in flight with a high-speed camera, you notice that they keep their heads very stable except in the most violent turns.

The parts of the inner ear that are important for orientation with respect to gravity are called the otolith organs: the utricle and the saccule. It is these parts of the inner ear that would be activated while the bat was hanging upside-down. Stimulating these parts of the inner ear, however, would not necessarily lead to dizziness, especially in a dark cave where there is no conflict between information from the inner-ear balance mechanism and vision.

But that's not all.

The way bats sense the world probably gives them immunity to dizziness.

When we humans move our heads around, our internal systems are giving us some information, but if you want to know where you are, you need your eyes. However, vision is very slow. Anything you look at takes a second or so to register in the brain.

Bats aren't blind, but they rely more on something called echolocation. Echolocation is a technique that some animals use to determine the location of things. They emit sound waves and listen for the echo. They use the delay to determine the distance. Using this method they are able to build up 3D images from echoes. Impressive, right?

Echolocating bats emit brief sonar chirps from 30 to more than 150 times per second (wow!) and respond to changes in echoes of less than a microsecond. Bats are working with a faster, more precise positioning system than humans do with vision.

So what does all this mean?

The bottom line is that bats are used to hanging upside-down without showing any behaviour that suggests dizziness. But because we cannot ask a bat directly whether or not it is dizzy, we'll never know for sure . . .

HOW TO FOSSILISE YOUR HAMSTER

Fossils are the remains of animals and plants that lived many, many years ago. Fossils are important to palaeontology or the study of prehistoric life because they give us clues about the animals that once roamed the earth, flew in the skies and swam in the seas — like the dinosaurs and the ichthyosaurs we mentioned earlier.

Most fossils are found in places that used to be underwater and they are usually formed from the hard parts of the animal – the bones, shells and teeth.

So what if you want to turn your beloved, recently deceased family pet into a fossil for the palaeontologists of the future to discover?

What do I need?
* a naturally deceased hamster (or other pet)
* a variety of environmental conditions

What do I do?
Take your hamster to one of the natural environments described below and ensure that it will not be removed from its final resting place by scavengers or natural phenomena.

What will I see?
Very little. Fossils take tens of thousands of years to form, but you will be saving up enjoyment for future generations.

What is (should be) going on?

A desire to preserve our fluffy pets' remains in fossilised form may be admirable, but the fact that they have a hard, mineralised skeleton and live a non-marine lifestyle is a bad start.

Conditions on the land make things tricky. The soft tissue surrounding the skeleton of mammals decays very quickly and it is usually preserved only if the animal dies at high altitude or in a freezing environment such as a glacial crevasse or in the polar regions, and then only in wizened, mummified form, which is not true fossilisation.

So, if you really want your pet to survive the ravages of geological time, then while it is still alive you need to concentrate on improving the quality of its teeth and bones. You can give your hamster a head-start in the fossilising process by feeding it a diet rich in calcium to build up its bones and teeth.

After that it's a matter of location, location, location. You need to bury your hamster somewhere it won't be disturbed for a very, very long time.

Fossilised remains are often found in caves, so you could ask your parents to take up potholing to scout out suitable locations (they'll need proper training, of course). Alternatively, you need to find a spot where your hamster will be buried quickly after it has been laid to rest – preferably somewhere natural and dramatic, the sort of site from which you can detect a distant volcanic rumble and clouds of ash being emitted skywards. Don't get too close though: an ash burial is good, incineration by flowing lava is not. Again, be very careful, you don't want to join your hamster in fossilised harmony at this stage.

Depending on where you live (and hopefully you don't live next to an active volcano or in a freezing glacier), you may have to travel a long distance to find the best place. A desert in the flash-flood season offers a good environment, as does a tropical river floodplain during heavy rain so you can bury your hamster in fine, oxygen-free mud.

However, the best environment to ensure a fossilised hamster is probably a sea burial in very deep water (shallow marine conditions are turbulent and full of life that will disturb or eat the remains). There are few creatures in the deep sea, and even fewer below the sediment and mud. As long as your hamster is not buried near a tectonic subduction zone where the Earth's crust is being consumed, such as the Pacific coast of the Americas, it should rest undisturbed until fossilisation takes place.

This environment and the land-bound ones described above are ideal. The oxygen-free conditions will slow decay of the body and the ash or fine seabed clay will help to preserve the body structure. Fossilisation will then proceed until your hamster is nothing more than an outline of carbon and petrified body fluids, thanks to compaction from the weight of sediment that settles above. You should allow at least 200,000 years for this.

Of course, there is more chance of winning the lottery than you or your pet ending up as a fossil, but that's no reason not to try . . .

How high can a butterfly fly?

Unlike humans, butterflies are not disposed to seeking altitude records. Indeed, they will not fly higher than is strictly necessary in their everyday lives, whether looking for a mate, food or somewhere to lay eggs, avoiding predators or migrating.

Worldwide there are many thousands of species of butterfly, each adapted to its own particular habitat and needs. Some spend their whole lives on a patch of coastal grassland, the larvae feeding on low plants or living in ants' nests, and the adults never flying more than a few feet above the ground. Others spend all their time in the tree canopy many metres above ground level.

Others are only found on high mountains. Even though they don't actually fly very high above the ground, butterflies that live on the mountains of Peru spend their whole lives at altitudes of around 6,000 metres.

Butterflies that migrate tend to fly the highest in general. The most famous migratory butterfly is probably the monarch, known to scientists as *Danaus plexippus*. These leave Mexico or California each year and fly north to Canada or the northern US, though actually it takes several generations to get there. Monarchs have been sighted by glider pilots flying as high as 1,200 metres. Interestingly, they seem to fly in the same way as a glider, using updraughts to gain sufficient altitude so that they can glide for quite a distance before needing to use energy to climb again.

Europe also has plenty of migratory species. The painted lady, *Vanessa cardui*, makes its way to southern France from north Africa; it has to leave Europe in winter because it can't survive a frost.

To get to France many will cross through the mountain passes of the Pyrenees, which in general lie at about 2,500 metres. During late summer and autumn these butterflies can be seen drifting southwards. If they encounter a high building, they just fly straight upwards and over it. If they encounter a high mountain range, they will do the same.

The mountain passes of the Caucasus are higher, while those of the Himalayas are higher still at 7,500 metres. But we wouldn't be surprised if migratory butterflies could fly straight over Everest if they encountered it in good weather.

However, insects of any kind cannot fly if they are too cold. Butterflies can keep warm by beating their wings, though if they fly too high in the wrong conditions, they may become too chilled.

On average, the air temperature reaches freezing at an altitude of just below 8,000 metres, suggesting that this would be their physical altitude limit. They might on occasion be carried higher on updraughts, but this surely doesn't count as autonomous flight.

Why don't polar bears' feet freeze?

If you've ever been playing in the snow and ended up with cold feet, you'll know how unpleasant it is. But hopefully you've never had to stand barefoot on ice. Polar bears do this all the time – so how come they don't freeze?

The reason is pretty simple: good insulation.

Polar bears are just about the best-insulated animals on the planet, certainly among those species of mammal that do not live primarily immersed in water. An adult bear has 10 centimetres of blubber beneath its skin, which in turn is covered by a thick coat of fur. This fur relies not only on its density, but also on its unique structure: each hair is a hollow tube, so that air is trapped inside the hairs as well as between them.

The polar bear also has very hairy pads on its feet, and the tough skin is extremely callused on the underside of the paws, so there is a sturdy layer of dead tissue between the ice and any blood vessels.

There may also be another factor at work. The underside of a polar bear's paw is dotted with dozens of papillae – small nipple-shaped extrusions of even more callused skin – which provide extra grip in the same way as the studs on a footballer's boot. It is these papillae that enable a polar bear to accelerate to a very respectable pace on the ice. They also prevent it skating out of control, past a potential meal.

On really cold, compacted ice, the bears tend to

lift part of the underside of the paw clear of the surface. The papillae enable an additional cushion of insulating air to be trapped between most of the pad and the ice.

But what about in summer?

A bear attempting a brisk trot in warmer temperatures of 10 °C or greater would quickly have a dangerous attack of heat stroke. Arctic summers can get much hotter than that, and that's bad news for the polar bear, which struggles to go about its daily life in warmer weather. And, if climate change continues to make the Arctic warmer, there's a good chance that the polar bear will die out.

🐙 WHY DO BOYS HAVE NIPPLES?

Why do dogs like jumping into cold ponds, while cats and humans generally do not?

Well, this is perhaps a question that confuses willingness with enjoyment.

Most dogs are prepared to dive into cold water, but we don't know if they actually *like* the experience. And when it comes to cats, the small fluffy ones that live in your house are different to the big ones that live in the wild.

But it's true: dogs don't mind cold water, while cats hate it. To understand why, we need to look at their respective evolutionary histories.

The dog (scientific name: *Canis lupus familiaris*) originated in central Asia during the aftermath of the last ice age, at least 15,000 years ago. It is descended from the grey wolf (*Canis lupus*), with all the evolutionary baggage that implies. Ice-age wolves preyed on sub-Arctic herd animals such as elk, reindeer and caribou, which would have migrated in search of better grazing, crossing fast-flowing rivers swollen by meltwater when required.

Any animal – including the ice-age wolves – swimming these rivers would have had to develop considerable physical and psychological resistance to low temperatures. Those that weren't prepared to get their feet wet wouldn't have lasted long enough to pass on their genes! Those that did survive handed down to their doggy descendants a tolerance for cold water.

Some 5,000 years after the big bad wolf began the transition to being man's best friend, a group of wild cats (*Felis sylvestris*) in what is now western Asia apparently attached themselves to the local human population. Significantly, the closest living relative of the proto-kitties is believed to be the sand cat (*Felis margarita*), an inhabitant of regions of extreme heat, such as the Sahara.

Having ancestors from the desert isn't likely to cultivate a tolerance for getting wet, whatever their temperature. Large mammals have no freshwater predators in the sub-Arctic, but animals originating in the tropics have good reasons for not going into the water – most of them possessing very powerful jaws . . . A prehistoric African waterhole was a fast-food outlet for large predators, both in and around the water.

A good way to see the different evolutionary journeys of cats and dogs is by watching our modern-day pets drink. A dog will generally lap up its water enthusiastically, albeit with the occasional sideways glance at any animal that could attack. A cat, on the other hand, displays far more caution, constantly looking around suspiciously and keeping its body as far back as possible from the liquid.

Why do some birds stand on one leg?

Some people think that the reason flamingos stand on one leg is so ducks don't swim into them as often! Nice idea, but the most likely answer has to do with conserving energy.

In cold weather, birds can lose a lot of heat through their legs because the blood vessels there are close to the surface. To reduce this, many species have a counter-current system of intertwined blood vessels so that blood from the body warms the cooler blood returning from the feet. Keeping one leg tucked inside their feathers and close to the warm body is another strategy to reduce heat loss.

In hot climates, blood in the legs will heat up quickly, so keeping one leg close to the body will reduce this effect and help the birds to maintain a stable body temperature.

Another factor in long-legged birds is that it may require significant work to pump blood back up the leg through narrow capillaries. Keeping the leg at a level closer to the heart may reduce this workload.

But don't they get pins and needles?

Birds' legs are structured differently to ours. What looks like the knee is in fact more like our ankle. Many birds have a mechanism to 'lock' the leg straight, so for them it is much easier to stand for hours on end on just one leg. Unless we want to fall over, we humans are better off standing on two.

Do penguins really fall over when they look up?

It's official: penguins don't fall over backwards when aircraft fly overhead.

So where did this rumour start?

British pilots came back from the 1982 Falklands War with stories of penguins toppling over. Concerned that increasing air traffic might endanger wildlife, a team led by Richard Stone of the British Antarctic Survey spent five weeks back in 2001 watching a thousand king penguins on South Georgia. But they were relieved to find out that, after numerous overflights by two Royal Navy Lynx helicopters, 'Not one king penguin fell over.' Phew.

Why aren't there any green mammals? Wouldn't that be useful for camouflage?

There is only one green mammal, the three-toed sloth.

Sloths are tree-dwelling mammals from Central and South America that are known for being very slow and sleeping a lot. Their greenness is a result of a coat of algae that covers their fur. The algae is thickest around their head and neck – where the fur is longest. Because sloths clean themselves with their hands and not their tongues, the algae-coating is never cleaned off.

Isn't this very annoying for the sloth?

Actually, it's very useful. One of the sloth's main predators is the eagle. There's no way that a sloth could move quicker than an eagle, but a green sloth that moves very slowly through the trees is very tricky to spot.

So the three-toed sloth isn't *really* green. In fact, there are no known mammals capable of producing their own green skin pigment.

The main reason for the absence of green mammals seems to be an ecological one. In general, mammals are simply too big to use a single colour for camouflage because there are no blocks of green large enough to conceal them. Most mammals have an environment that is made up of patches of light and dark and composed of many different colours. This means that those mammals that are camouflaged tend to be dappled or striped. Animals that do use green coloration for camouflage, such as frogs and lizards, are small enough to use solid blocks of green – leaves and foliage – for cover.

The main predators of most mammals are other mammals, especially the carnivores, such as the cat, dog and weasel families. Carnivores are all colour-blind or, at best, have very limited colour vision. Hence effective camouflage against them is not a matter of coloration but of a combination of factors such as brightness, texture, pattern and movement.

Why do fish fart?

In 2003, biologists linked a mysterious underwater farting sound to bubbles coming out of a herring fish's bottom. No fish had been known before to emit sound from its backside or to be capable of producing such a high-pitched noise.

'It sounds just like a high-pitched raspberry,' said Ben Wilson, then at the University of British Columbia in Vancouver, Canada. Wilson and his colleagues could not be sure why herring made this sound, but initial research suggested that it might explain the puzzle of how shoals keep together after dark.

Scientists were excited to discover that fish farting might be used for communication.

Fish are known to call out to potential mates with low grunts and buzzes, produced by wobbling a balloon of air called the swim bladder located in their tummies. The swim bladder inflates and deflates to adjust the fish's buoyancy.

The biologists initially assumed that the high-pitched sound they had detected was also coming from the swim bladder in the fish's stomach, but then they noticed that a stream of bubbles expelled from the fish's bottom corresponded exactly with the timing of the noise . . .

Because the scientists needed a more important-sounding name than 'fish farts', they decided to call the noise Fast Repetitive Tick (FRT – which is a bit like fart).

Unlike a human fart, the sounds were probably not caused by digestive gases because the number of sounds did not change when the fish were fed. The researchers also tested whether the fish were farting from fear, perhaps to sound an alarm, but when they exposed fish to a shark scent, there was again no change in the number of farts.

So what was all this fish farting about?

Three things persuaded the researchers that the fish farts were most likely to be produced for communication. Firstly, when more herring were in a tank, the researchers recorded more farts per fish. Secondly, the herring were only noisy after dark, indicating that the sounds might allow the fish to locate one another when they could not be seen. Thirdly, the biologists knew that herring could hear sounds of this frequency, while most other fish cannot. This would allow them to communicate by farting without alerting predators to their presence.

It's just a theory for now, but the discovery means that one day scientists might be able to track fish by their farts in the same way that whales and dolphins are monitored by their high-pitched squeals.

Why do scientists collect whale poo?

'I hope we get a poop today,' said Rosalind Rolland, a conservationist then at the New England Aquarium, pouring her morning tea. 'Just one.'

'Maybe two,' said her colleague Scott Kraus. 'If you follow something long enough, it'll poop.'

Their colleague Fargo, having dedicated over half his life to the subject, was even more enthusiastic. In 2006, Fargo was one of an elite corps of whale-poo sniffer dogs, and perhaps the most important member of the research team.

Whales may be the biggest creatures on the planet, but they also swim fast and dive deep, so are notoriously difficult to study. Fortunately, you can tell a lot about an animal by studying what it leaves behind. In whale poo, researchers can find clues about where whales are, about how many of them there are, about how they reproduce and about their stress levels, health and vitality. There's a lot you can do with poo.

Spotting poo samples, which hang just below the sea's surface before they break apart, is far more difficult than finding the animals themselves. That's where dogs like Fargo come in. With years of training and more than 200 million olfactory receptors in their noses – compared with humans' mere 5 million – dogs are expert poo-collectors.

Upwind of a few whales, Fargo dropped his snout. 'He's got scent,' said Rolland. Fargo paced back and forth across the bow but then stopped moving. He had lost the scent. 'It might have just been a big fart,' Rolland conceded.

Rolland figured that poo sampling would help her narrow down why these whales, known as right whales, had stopped reproducing in the North Atlantic in the late 1990s. She thought faecal samples could be used to test reproductive hormones, as had been done in primates and other animals. They began with just humans searching for whale poo, but when dogs were introduced samples increased fourfold. On average, dogs collected about one poo an hour – a rate Rolland referred to as 'poops per unit effort'.

I bet you're imagining that whale poo is huge, right?

Well it isn't – it's actually surprisingly small, about the size of a small brick and a reddish-brown colour.

When the team finally located one, research assistant Cindy Browning scooped it up into a net. Once it was brought on board, the smell was overwhelming. 'If you spill it on your clothes,' Rolland warned, 'you want to throw those clothes away.'

But the smell was worth it because the samples were proving really, really useful. Rolland and her colleagues showed that various factors might have been to blame for the whale's failure to recover from centuries of hunting. Eating contaminated shellfish may have been to blame, but the scientists also found something even more troubling: parasites that cause disease in land mammals.

How did the land parasites get into the sea-dwelling whales? The blame might lie with humans. These whales spend much of their lives close to big cities, so they might have been picking up these parasites from human or domestic animal waste dumped in the ocean.

But it wasn't all bad news. Hormone studies suggested that the female right whales were doing well, so there was hope for more whale babies.

The study had also been expanded to study killer whales, or orcas, whose poos are a snotty greenish brown. Orca poo is less buoyant than right whale poo, so it is difficult to spot from a boat.

. . . and why do they collect whale snot, too?

What is the strangest thing you could do with a remote-controlled toy helicopter? Strapping on a few Petri dishes and flying it through whale snot must be high on the list.

But this is how Karina Acevedo-Whitehouse, a veterinarian and conservation biologist then with the Zoological Society of London, has spent much of her time.

In 2008, Acevedo-Whitehouse made it possible to study the viruses, fungi and bacteria that hitch a ride in whale lungs for the first time.

It's pretty easy to take blood samples from other marine mammals, such as seals and sea lions. But a whale's sheer bulk means that such a sampling would probably be fatal for any veterinarian. So Acevado-Whitehouse decided to go after their snot instead.

She first tried tying herself to a research boat and leaning overboard to catch a bit of whale snot in Petri dishes. 'It worked,' she said, 'but it wasn't very safe.'

Then she came up with a better solution. For species like grey and sperm whales that did not mind being close to a boat, the researchers attached their Petri dishes to a long pole and held them out over the blows.

With the shyer blue whale, her team had to resort to miniature helicopters. The Petri dishes were attached beneath the metre-long choppers, which were remotely flown through whale snot. 'The whales definitely notice the helicopter,' said Acevedo-Whitehouse, 'they turn on their sides to look at it. But they don't seem bothered and we don't even touch them.'

Now she and other researchers are using custom-built drones to collect whale snot.

Do mosquitoes get malaria? Do rats catch bubonic plague? If not, why not?

Rats can get quite sick from plague fleas and some will die, but usually not too quickly. Plague-carrying rats are at their most dangerous when they are about to die, because their fleas leave them as soon as they are dead to find new hosts.

When it comes to mosquitoes, the picture is more complicated.

The malaria parasite is called *Plasmodium*. It does not usually kill its host mosquitoes, though it may take a high enough toll on the mosquito's health that it is better for the insect not to get infected.

If we could breed mosquitoes that were resistant to the parasite we might find that they outcompete ordinary mosquitoes, and this might ultimately help get rid of malaria. But this kind of strategy would not work with another disease caused by mosquitoes, yellow fever, because the virus hardly seems to affect the mosquitoes.

Farmer Buckley's exploding trousers

Richard Buckley was lucky. When his trousers blew up, he wasn't wearing them. He was badly shocked, but his quick thinking saved him from serious injury.

It was a pretty normal August day in 1931, when Farmer Buckley's trousers were drying in front of the fire. Then, suddenly, they exploded. Although he was stunned by the force of the explosion, he grabbed the garments and threw them out of the house, where they exploded more on the front lawn.

There was only one suspect in the case: sodium chlorate.

Until recently, the chemical had been more familiar to men who worked in the quarry than to farmers, but when government scientists declared it the best ragwort killer they had seen, farmers began clamouring for it.

Buckley lived and farmed in Taranaki, which is on the western side of the North Island of New Zealand. He was just one of a growing number of people who got more than they bargained for with the miracle new weedkiller.

Ragwort, known to plant experts as *Senecio jacobaea*, was accidentally introduced to New Zealand in the late nineteenth century and quickly became a pest. By the 1920s, the weed was rampant. What made matters worse was that at this time there was a massive shift from sheep farming to dairying, and ragwort was particularly dangerous for cows.

Ragwort contains lots of nasty things: it is so toxic that even honey made from its flowers is poisonous. Livestock usually avoid the plant, but once it displaces grass and clover the animals have little else to eat. Sheep can eat it for months before showing signs of illness, but cattle and horses sicken quickly and can die of liver failure.

The boom in dairy farming followed the arrival of new technology — first refrigerated ships, then motor vehicles and machines to separate cream from milk. The first refrigerated ships began to carry produce to the UK in 1882. At first they took mainly meat. Shipments of dairy produce only took off once motor vehicles began to replace horses, allowing farmers to get fresh milk to the local dairy factory. When farmers began to separate the cream themselves, the butter factories introduced collection rounds, picking up the cream from the farm gate. As demand and factories grew, dairy farms spread into remote areas once thought too out-of-the-way to bother with. Between 1899 and 1919, the number of dairy cows doubled. Over the next two decades it doubled again.

In the past, farmers had grubbed up ragwort by hand, a labour-intensive job that brought only temporary relief: any roots left in the soil simply re-sprouted. But hands were becoming hard to find. Even the unemployed thought that the work was too hard and the pay was too low. By the late 1920s, farmers couldn't even turn to their families: it wasn't respectable to send your wife to work in the fields, and now that school had become compulsory (and there were buses to collect children from the farms and inspectors with cars to check on any who didn't turn up) you couldn't rope in your children either.

So farmers were desperate and prepared to consider any method of getting rid of ragwort.

The first the farmers heard of the weedkiller was in 1930, when a scientist at the Department of Agriculture wrote an article promising that it would 'completely destroy all the plants'. The farmers listened.

Within a year, everyone was desperate to get their hands on this miracle weedkiller. But the accidents started immediately. Mixed with organic material such as the fibres of a farmer's working clothes, sodium chlorate is extremely dangerous, forming compounds that will detonate at the first sign of a spark or a glowing cigarette. Sometimes just a shock or a knock is enough. Washing contaminated clothes made little difference.

By the time Buckley's trousers hit the headlines in Taranaki, farmers must have known of the dangers of sodium chlorate. But farmers needed something, and they continued to use the weedkiller until the late 1930s, when word got around that sodium chlorate wasn't as effective as the government scientists had promised.

Nearly a century later, farmers are still looking for a solution. Ragwort remains a serious pest in New Zealand. Today's weapons of choice are not herbicides but insects, the plant's natural enemies in its native Europe. The ragwort flea beetle was introduced in the early 1980s and has been very successful in some parts of New Zealand. However, the beetles didn't like the wetter climate of western New Zealand, so scientists are now looking at moths, whose caterpillars attack ragwort's roots.

Insects may prove the much-needed miracle cure – but this time round, scientists are keeping a more careful watch and a tighter rein on them.

FOOD
AND
DRINK

"NO DESSERT UNTIL you've had your dinner."
We've all heard it before, but have you ever
wondered why adults always tell you to eat savoury
food before sweet food?

Wouldn't it be simpler if there was just a single
food that could provide all the nutrients you need
to stay healthy? If only it were cake . . .

Although maybe not the cake that's featured in
this chapter – that's the oldest cake in the world.
We find out just how old it is and, more
importantly, if it's still edible.

If that hasn't whetted your appetite, or you just
want a scientific reason to play with your food, this
chapter also shows you how to kill a banana,
extract iron from your cereal and make green eggs
(minus the ham). Delicious!

Is there a single foodstuff that could provide all the nutrients that a human needs to stay reasonably healthy indefinitely?

Any single substance such as water or fat? No.

Any single tissue such as potato? No.

But considering we must be allowed to continue drinking water and breathing air (even though those are also nutrients), we can relax our rules a bit.

Not surprisingly, no strict monodiet can rival any healthily balanced diet, but there are two classes of foodstuffs that in appropriate quantities can maintain a reasonable level of health.

One such class is baby food. Some baby foods contain eggs, milk, certain seeds, and so on. Not as tasty as pizza and no single baby food is a perfect option, but some are adequate.

The other – and you might consider this a cheat – is whole animals. Oysters or fish such as whitebait or sardines might supply the necessary nutrient uptake. Animals sufficiently closely related to humans might also do, if eaten in the correct form and quantity. Farming families in the semidesert Karoo region of South Africa apparently ate mainly sheep or cattle.

For the most perfectly balanced human monodiet, however, other humans would be the logical food of choice. Not sure there would be many takers though – and we certainly aren't encouraging it!

HOW TO KILL A BANANA WITH COLD

This is counterintuitive to those of us brought up to believe that chilling foodstuffs slows decay, but a simple experiment will show us if it's true or not.

What do I need?

* two or more bananas (and possibly some fresh banana skins)
* a fridge (and possibly a domestic freezer)
* lemon juice

What do I do?

Place one banana in the fridge and leave the other at room temperature (approx. 20 °C). Observe each banana three or four times a day and note the relative discoloration of the skins. As a side-experiment, rub a third banana with lemon juice before subjecting it to the fridge conditions.

What will I see?

The banana in the fridge will brown or blacken faster than the one at room temperature. However, a banana rubbed with lemon juice and placed in the fridge will not decay at the same rate as the untreated one.

What's going on?

While many fruits are stabilised by refrigeration, most tropical and subtropical fruits, and bananas in particular, just can't handle the cold.

Tests show that the ideal temperature for bananas is 13.3 °C. Below 10 °C, the browning that normally happens as they decay is accelerated because their cells' internal membranes are damaged, releasing enzymes and other substances. Banana skin can blacken overnight as it softens and breaks down.

What's happening is that the membranes that keep the contents of the various compartments inside a cell separate are essentially two layers of slippery fat molecules or lipids. Chill these membranes and they get stickier and less flexible. If you chill the fruit too much, areas of the membranes become too sticky, the membranes collapse and enzymes and other molecules that are normally kept apart mix and kick off chemical reactions that speed up the softening of the fruit.

The skin goes black because of the action of an enzyme called polyphenol oxidase. The enzyme encourages the breakdown of smelly compounds called phenols in the banana skin. This produces substances similar to the pigment melanin that gives human skin and hair its colour. Just as when you get out in the sun, the amount of melanin increases in your skin, giving you a tan, as the banana breaks down, its skin gets darker.

The change in colour starts sooner in refrigerated bananas because, when the cold makes the membranes collapse, the molecules mix earlier than they would have done through normal decay.

The cold itself does not speed up the browning part of the reaction, it just starts it off earlier. In fact, once your banana is damaged by the cold in the fridge, if you take it out again the browning process will speed up because the reaction that causes the browning, once it is under way, is speeded up by heat.

This can be demonstrated by putting a banana skin in a freezer for a few hours. The inner surface will stay creamy white because, although the membranes are destroyed by the freezing process, the oxidases cannot work at such low temperatures. Then let it thaw overnight at room temperature. In the morning, it will be pitch-black due to the damage the membranes suffered in the freezer. Had the cold itself caused the blackening, it would have turned dark while it was being frozen.

Decay can be slowed by acids, which prevent the release of the polyphenol oxidase enzyme. This is why adding lemon juice — which is rich in citric acid — to skins can slow the blackening process. A similar slowing of the breakdown process can be seen if bananas are coated in wax; this stops oxygen reaching the skin and speeding up decay.

HOW TO MAKE GREEN EGGS

Dr Seuss would like this one.

With just a small amount of red cabbage juice — and an adult to help you — you can change the colour of fried eggs from white to green.

What do I need?
* shredded red cabbage (boiled for 20 minutes)
* a frying pan
* oil
* one egg

What do I do?

Squeeze the juice from the cooled cooked cabbage into a jug. Heat the oil in a frying pan, begin to fry the egg until the white is just turning from clear to white. Drip a small amount of cabbage juice into the setting egg white.

What will I see?

The egg white will turn lurid green where the juice hits it.

What's going on?

Red cabbage juice is a good indicator of whether a substance is an alkali or an acid. If added to an alkali, such as ammonia, it will turn green; if added to an acid, such as lemon juice, it will turn red. In neutral substances it is purple, the natural colour of red cabbage.

Because egg white (mostly the protein albumen) is alkaline, it turns green.

The experiment works because red cabbage contains water-soluble pigments called anthocyanins (also found in plums, apple skins and grapes). These change colour depending on whether they are in the presence of an acid or an alkali. This explains why red cabbage that is pickled turns red, rather than its natural purple colour. Pickling takes place in vinegar, which is acidic.

PS: Another fun thing you can do at home is create 'magic' paper. Soak cheap, absorbent paper in boiled red cabbage water and leave it to dry. Then paint it with household substances such as vinegar, orange juice or washing powder dissolved in water. A range of colours will appear depending on the acidic or alkaline nature of the 'paints'.

Why is frozen milk yellow?

The yellow colour of frozen milk comes from a vitamin called riboflavin, which actually got its name from its colour — flavus is the Latin for yellow.

Riboflavin is dissolved in the watery portion of milk, which is also filled with minute particles of protein and droplets of butterfat. In fresh milk, all the suspended particles and droplets scatter any light that strikes them evenly, so that the milk appears opaque and white — milky, in other words.

However, as the milk freezes, most of its water crystallises into ice before other substances freeze. So the normally dilute riboflavin becomes concentrated in the remaining liquid water. This means these areas start to turn yellow and, as the clear water-ice crystals form, we are able to see it.

HOW TO EXTRACT IRON FROM YOUR BREAKFAST CEREAL

Breakfast cereals often claim to be fortified with iron. Well, are they?

They are and, more amazingly, if you have a magnet you can extract it too! So ponder the ingredients list on your packet of cornflakes while you are munching breakfast, and then set about removing one of them . . .

What do I need?
* breakfast cereal fortified with iron (cornflakes work, but check on the side of the packet to see what the iron content is — the higher, the better)
* a plastic cup
* a spoon or pestle to crush the cereal (better still, a blender)
* hot water

* a very strong magnet
* clean white paper
* a clear, sealable plastic sandwich bag

What do I do?

Fill the cup to about two-thirds full with cereal, and with the spoon or pestle crush the cereal into a fine powder. It is worth spending a lot of time on this stage – the finer the powder, the better.

Put the crushed cereal into the sandwich bag and add hot water. Leave the mixture for about 15 to 20 minutes. Now gently tilt the bag forward so that the cereal collects on one side, and place the magnet along the outside of the bag near the cereal, running it over the bottom, because the iron tends to sink. Tilt the bag back so that the cereal runs away from the magnet. You can also lay the bag flat on the table and stroke it with the magnet towards one corner.

Alternatively, if you are using a blender, put the cereal straight into the blender and add hot water until the cereal is submerged. Wait for about 15 to 20 minutes until the cereal is soft, then blend it all together. While the blender is whirring, place the magnet on the outside of the blender near the mixture, and keep it there as you turn the blender off.

What will I see?

The magnet will attract a black fuzz of iron. Move the magnet over the surface of the bag or blender and the tiny pieces of iron will follow it.

What's going on?

The black stuff in your cereal really is iron – the same stuff that is found in nails and trains and motorbikes. And it's quite heavy, which is why you need to make sure you run your magnet along the bottom of the cup. The iron is added to the mix when the cereals are being made and you really do eat it when you devour your cornflakes.

The reason it is added in a form that you can extract is that iron ions (iron that would more easily combine with other molecules in the cereal) would increase the spoilage rate of the food. Using iron in its pure metal form gives the cereal a longer shelf-life. The hydrochloric acid and other chemicals in your stomach dissolve some of this iron and it is absorbed through your digestive tract, although much of it remains untouched and comes out in the loo.

Humans need iron for many important bodily functions. Red blood cells carry haemoglobin, of which iron is a key constituent. Haemoglobin transports oxygen through the blood to the rest of the body by binding oxygen to its iron atom and carrying it through the bloodstream. As our red blood cells are being replaced constantly, iron is an essential part of our diet.

Why do we have to eat savoury foods before sweet foods?

Ever wish you could skip straight to dessert?

The idea of having a savoury dinner before a sweet dessert is unique to humans. Our pets are happy with just one bowl of food.

Most animals from microbes to hunter-gatherers eat what they can when they can. Given a choice, they proceed from their favourite items to the necessary evils. The more prized the food, the higher the probability of losing it through procrastination, so they eat the best bits first.

Even today, children will go for the goodies first when they can.

Only once humans had achieved security, productivity and the leisure time for multiple-course meals did they come up with the idea of having two different plates of food. Long before people discovered that flooding the blood with sugar is an unhealthy habit, they had learned that sweet foods fill you up, and so should be saved until the end.

HOW TO MAKE YOUR TEETH FEEL WEIRD (USING SPINACH)

This works better with canned spinach than with fresh, but since spinach is so good for you, you can try with both.

What do I need?
* plenty of spinach leaves (preferably canned, heat-processed spinach)
* a pan of boiling water
* a colander
* a plate
* a fork

What do I do?

Ask an adult to boil the spinach until it is cooked, drain it, let it cool a little. Then it's over to you. Eat it and then run your tongue around your teeth and mouth.

What will I feel?

Your teeth and the inside of your mouth will feel fuzzy and furry. Yuck.

What's going on?

Spinach contains a large amount of oxalate crystals – mineral salts of oxalic acid. When spinach is cooked – especially the canned variety – some of the spinach cell wall structure is damaged and the oxalate crystals leak out. These coat your mouth to give the fuzzy feeling and it explains why fresh, uncooked spinach does not produce a similar effect. Spinach is also rich in calcium and oxalic acid, and these combine with the calcium in saliva to deposit large amounts of furry, calcium-rich plaque on your teeth.

PS: Chard and beetroot leaves have a similar effect.

How old is the oldest cake in the world? (And can you still eat it?)

It's always sad when you go to eat your favourite sweet treat only to discover it is out of date. But things could be much worse.

Take the case of Fidelia Bates of Tecumseh, Michigan. After baking a fruit cake for Thanksgiving in the late 1870s, she promptly died. This presented a rather delicate question for the family: who would be the first to eat a piece of the dead woman's cake?

As it turned out, nobody would, at least not for a long, long time

Mrs Bates's family has resisted temptation to polish it off for over 140 years, and counting. 'It's hard, it's crystallised, it's fossilised,' said her great-grandson Morgan Ford. 'Nobody wanted to eat it after she passed away, and so now I have it.'

The cake has been kept under a glass lid and stored high up in a cupboard ever since, save for the occasional appearance on TV or at Morgan's grandchildren's school show-and-tell.

The fruit cake has attracted a few daredevils over the years. 'My uncle was the first to try a tiny piece off it, about twenty-five years ago,' said Ford. 'And I did lift the lid off when it turned a hundred and for a moment we could smell rum.'

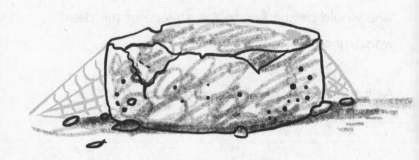

This cake isn't the only old food to be reported in the newspapers.

In 1951, Mrs E. Burt Phillips of West Hanover, Massachusetts, returned a 56-year-old can of clams to the manufacturer ('still edible', the press duly reported). A year later a 70-year-old crock of butter ('still white and sweet') was retrieved from an abandoned well in Illinois. In 1968, Sylvia Rapson of Cowley, UK, found a loaf of bread baked in 1896, still edible, tightly wrapped in table linen in an attic trunk ('I'm keeping it for sentimental reasons,' she informed *The Times*), and when a house in Grimsby was razed to the ground in 1970, the ruins miraculously yielded up a 1928 packet of breakfast cereal – a find that was declared, inevitably, 'still edible'.

But if you found a bit of food this old, would you eat it?

In 1969, a man called George Lambert did just that. He turned up at the New Mexico state fair wearing his uniform from the 1898 Spanish–American war. Inside his mess kit he found a piece of hard tack, a long-lasting biscuit, and to the crowd's awe he bit a piece off and ate it. 'Tastes just like it did then,' the grizzled veteran announced. 'Wasn't any good then and it isn't now.'

Oscar Pike, a food scientist at Brigham Young University in Provo, Utah, would probably not have been surprised. Having conducted taste and odour tests on everything from 30-year-old dried milk to oatmeal, Pike announced his results: the oatmeal wasn't all that good, but not all that bad either. When Pike was asked which old food he would eat himself he said '30-year-old wheat. Baked into wholewheat bread it has practically the same sensory quality as bread made from freshly grown wheat.'

Grains are known for their longevity. In March 2006, 352,000 vitamin-fortified crackers from the Cold War turned up in a forgotten vault below the Brooklyn Bridge. A New York bridge inspector, sampling one, said they had 'a unique flavour'.

If you did eat a cracker as old as your grandfather, would you get sick?

In the case of dried foods, the answer generally seems to be no. But then, why would you want to?

HOW TO TRICK YOUR FRIENDS INTO THINKING THEY ARE EATING SOMETHING OTHER THAN WHAT'S IN THEIR MOUTHS

Is it true that you can fool yourself into believing you are eating something other than the food that's in your mouth?

Yes: try it on yourself and then use it as a prank on your friends . . .

What do I need?

* a sliced apple
* a sliced pear
* your nose
* your mouth

What do I do?

Hold a piece of the pear under your nose while eating a slice of the apple.

What will I taste?

Despite the fact that you are eating apple, you'll think you are eating pear.

What's going on?

The confusion arises in part because most people think that they taste using their taste buds. They don't.

We all detect flavours via our sense of smell. Indeed, most of what we call taste is actually flavour produced by the smell of food passing from our mouths into our nasal cavities where we detect it through our sense of smell. True taste is only the bitter, sweet, salt, sour and umami (savoury) detected by the taste buds.

When you bite into a strawberry, your tongue only tells you that it is sweet, just as it would if it were chocolate. It's the odours rising through your throat to your nose that tell you that that particular sweetness is strawberry-flavoured.

If you remove the sense of smell or block those odours, or – as in the experiment above – replace them with something else, you can confuse your senses of taste and smell. Your taste buds detect the apple in your mouth as being sweetly acidic using its sweet- and sour-detecting taste buds, and your sense of touch recognises the texture to be that of a type of tree fruit.

However, because you can more strongly detect the smell of pear under your nose than you can the flavour of apple rising through the back of your mouth, your brain is fooled into thinking that what's in your mouth is a piece of pear. The experiment works best this way round because pears have a stronger smell than apples.

So it's easy to fool our senses?

Yes, and there are some people who have a condition called synaesthesia who make bizarre sense associations all the time. No one is really certain, but this condition is thought to involve crossed wires in the brain.

We are born with many connections between different areas of our brain, but as we get older, continually using our brain, new connections are made and our brain cuts back on those connections it doesn't need. Synaesthetic connections are possibly some of the early ones that should have been pruned out during infancy.

The extraordinary result is that some people – as many as 1 in 25 – perceive things like letters, words, numbers or days of the week as having very distinct and immutable colours. A smaller group even experience sounds as having colour or tastes as having shapes. One member of this group was reported as saying that she knew when the milk was about to go off because she perceived that its shape had begun to quiver!

The great tooth robbery

The night of 18 June 1815 was one to remember. After 23 years of war in Europe, Napoleon faced the combined might of Britain, Holland and Prussia at Waterloo. By 10 p.m., the battle was over. The French were defeated and 50,000 men lay dead or wounded on the battlefield. The casualties were high – but for one group of people that was reason to celebrate. For dentists this was the great tooth bonanza.

Waterloo was a well-timed battle. It was dark by the end of the fighting and the battlefield scavengers could go about their work unseen. In the gloom, shadowy figures flitted from corpse to corpse, gathering up the soldiers' weapons and winkling out any valuables tucked inside their torn and bloodied uniforms. Then came the final act of desecration: with expertise many a dental surgeon might envy, they deftly pulled and pocketed any intact front teeth.

Taking teeth from the dead to replace those lost by the living was nothing new. But this time the scale of it was different. The flood of teeth onto the market was so huge that dentures made from second-hand teeth acquired a new name: Waterloo teeth.

But surely no one would want a dead soldier's teeth?

Actually, they did. They really did.

Far from putting clients off, this was a positive selling point. Better to have teeth from a relatively fit and healthy young man killed by a cannonball or sabre than incisors plucked from the jaws of a disease-riddled corpse decaying in the grave or from a hanged man left dangling too long on the gibbet.

So how bad were the false teeth back then?

Until the eighteenth century, false teeth were made in much the same way as they had been since the sixth century BC. Back then, the most skilled manufacturers of dental prosthetics were the Etruscans. They did a fantastic line in gold bridgework. Depending on the size of the gap, they made a series of gold hoops. The outer ones fitted around the nearest sound teeth, and the rest were filled with artificial teeth carved from ivory or bone and riveted in place with a gold pin. These not only looked impressive, they were secure enough to eat with.

But the same can't be said of many later designs.

In the late eighteenth and early nineteenth centuries people dreaded losing their teeth: the toothless had sunken cheeks and looked old before their time. Without teeth, it was hard for people to understand you. Toothless people tended to keep their mouths shut rather than reveal their naked gums.

For those who could afford it, the answer was a set of false teeth. But dentures rarely fitted, looked nothing like the real thing and in most cases weren't secure enough to risk eating with.

Some sets of teeth were carved from a single piece of ivory or bone. In the more sophisticated designs, artificial teeth were riveted to a plate made of ox bone or hippo ivory, and the teeth were carved from the same material.

The biggest drawback of all was that decay soon set in and the result was a rotten taste in the mouth and evil-smelling breath. You might have seen paintings of the olden days where women were carrying fans – this fashion was prompted by the all-too-common need to hide bad teeth and stinking breath.

Dentures made from human teeth were better. They looked better, resisted wear and kept their colour longer – but they were still liable to decay and eventually needed replacing.

What dentists wanted more than anything was a steady supply of human teeth. They could never get enough, so teeth were very expensive. In

1781, Paul Jullion of Gerrard Street in London was charging half a guinea (about £90 nowadays) for a single artificial tooth, and four times that for a human one. A row of artificial upper teeth cost £20 and 10 shillings. The real thing fetched £31 and 10 shillings (That's the equivalent of about £5,500 nowadays).

Sometimes the poor could be persuaded to part with good teeth. In 1783, a dentist advertised in a New York newspaper, offering 2 guineas each for sound teeth. But people had to be desperate to sell their teeth.

The dead needed no persuading. Teeth from the battlefield were the best you could hope for – but it wasn't always what people got.

Many second-hand teeth came from mortuaries, the dissecting room and the gallows (where criminals had been hanged to death). Some people stole corpses from the graveyards in order to sell bits of the bodies to medical schools. These people were called 'resurrectionists'.

Before the Battle of Waterloo, the Peninsular War had bolstered supplies. Tooth hunters followed the armies, moving in as soon as the living had left the field. There were so many spare teeth that they were shipped abroad by the barrel. In 1819, American dentist Levi Spear Parmly, the inventor of floss, wrote that he had 'in his possession thousands of teeth extracted from bodies of all ages that have fallen in battle'.

By this time, the first porcelain teeth had begun to appear. Initially they were too white, too brittle and made a horrid grating noise. Then, in 1837, London denture maker Claudius Ash — driven by his hatred of handling dead men's teeth — perfected porcelain dentures and began to manufacture them commercially.

Even so, trade in the real thing continued well into the second half of the century. Some London dentists refused to switch to porcelain. Plus, they now had a whole new source: on the other side of the Atlantic, the tooth robbers were hard at work, cleaning up behind the armies of the American Civil War.

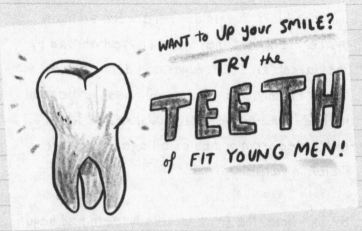

EARTH
AND
SPACE

WHEN DO ASTRONAUTS eat their sandwiches? *Launch time, of course!*

Have you ever wondered about the practicalities of being an astronaut? Going to the toilet isn't so easy in a spaceship, and what on Earth – pun intended – do you do with a pair of dirty pants when you are orbiting the planet at 17,000 mph?

If going to space is a little too far, you can conduct your own scientific experiments without having to leave the house. This chapter shows you how to improve your eyesight, measure the speed of light using just a chocolate bar and a microwave, and how to create an explosion with just some sweets and a fizzy drink. You might want to venture outside for that last one, it can get rather messy!

Where on our planet is the furthest point from any sea?

The furthest point from the sea is called the continental pole of inaccessibility (CPI). There are a few possible candidate sites, depending on what you count as coastline, but the most famous one is located at 46° 17' N, 86° 40' E, in the Dzoosotoyn Elisen in Xinjiang, China, and is about 2,645 kilometres from the nearest coastline, at Tianjin on the Yellow Sea.

Although people had worked out where it was a long time ago, it wasn't visited by surveyor-explorers until 27 June 1986. The first people there were British cousins Nicholas Crane and Richard Crane. The Cranes travelled there by bicycle, crossing the Hindu Kush and Gobi Desert, to raise funds for a charity that supports technological advances in developing countries.

So what's it like there?

 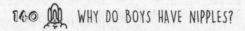

The summers are very hot and the winters are very, very cold.

Why is this?

The huge temperature difference is because the region is so far from the ocean. Every day the sun warms up the land quickly (which also warms the air above it) and every night it cools quickly. But water is said to have a high heating capacity because it takes much longer to warm up and cool down. That means that water and the air above it stay at a more constant temperature during the day and night. This helps keep land that is close to the sea at a more constant temperature. This means that the farther a region is from the ocean, the more extreme its climate is likely to be. And the CPI is as far from the sea as you can get.

'Elisen' means 'desert' in a local dialect, and this part of Xinjiang might be considered an extension of the Gobi Desert. Temperatures in the desert can drop to -40 °C in winter. At the other extreme, during daytime in summer it can reach a blistering 50 °C. Temperatures can vary by as much as 32 °C within a 24-hour period!

So if you want to go and visit the CPI you should pack your swimming trunks and suncream – and your winter coat!

HOW TO MEASURE THE SPEED OF LIGHT USING A CHOCOLATE BAR AND A MICROWAVE

This is an amazing experiment that actually allows you to measure one of the fundamentals of science – the speed of light – in your own home!

What do I need?
* a bar of chocolate (the longer the better)
* a ruler
* a microwave oven

What do I do?

Remove the turntable from your microwave oven – the bar of chocolate needs to be stationary. Put the chocolate in the microwave and cook at high power until it starts to melt in two or three spots – this usually takes about 40 seconds. You should stop after 60 seconds maximum, for safety.

What will I see?

Because the chocolate is not rotating, the microwaves the oven produces are not evenly distributed throughout the bar and spots of chocolate will begin to melt in the high-intensity areas or 'hotspots'. Remove the bar from the microwave and measure the distance between globs of melted chocolate.

What's going on?

Microwave ovens get their name from the waves they use to cook food with: a form of electro-magnetic radiation (just like light) called – wait for it – microwaves. These race through the air

at the speed of light in a wavelike fashion of
peaks and troughs.

The number of waves per second, also known as
the frequency, is the key here. A standard oven
will probably have a frequency of 2.45 gigahertz
(the figure should be given on the back of the
oven or in the instruction manual). If your oven is
2.45 GHz, this means the microwaves oscillate
2,450,000,000 times a second (you can adjust
this figure depending on your particular oven). So
now you know how frequently the waves go up and
down, you just need to know the distance between
the peaks of the waves, which is known as the
wavelength. That will help you to calculate how
fast they are travelling.

This is where the chocolate comes in. Because the
wave will melt the chocolate when it goes through
it on the upward part of the wave and the
downward part, the distance between the globs of
molten chocolate is half the wavelength of the
microwaves in your oven. So double the
measurement you have taken of the gap between

the molten globs to find the microwave wavelength. In the *New Scientist* microwave oven, the distance between the globs of molten chocolate was 6 cm, so the wavelength in our 2.45 GHz oven is 12 cm.

To calculate the speed of light in centimetres per second you need to multiply this wavelength by the frequency of the microwaves. So you do 12 * 2,450,000,000 = 29,400,000,000, which is astoundingly near to the true speed of light of 29,979,245,800cm per second (or 299,792,458 m per second as it is usually expressed).

Try it yourself, measuring as accurately as possible to get a figure even nearer to the true speed. If your chocolate bar is chilled beforehand, the molten areas tend to be more distinct when they first appear. Of course, you may find that a variety of different chocolate bars, all of which taste delicious slightly melted, will aid your research. True scientists know that it is always important to double-check results.

Why can't we point one of our space telescopes at the moon to prove that humans landed there?

On 20 July 1969, *Apollo 11* became the first crewed spacecraft to land on the moon. It had a crew of three American astronauts: Neil Armstrong, Buzz Aldrin and Michael Collins. Neil Armstrong was the first to walk on the moon (the original moonwalk!), famously saying 'That's one small step for man, one giant leap for mankind'.

All around the world, people watched this important historical moment on their black and white televisions. There were 600 million people watching.

The mission was part of the Space Race, a competition of space exploration between the Soviet Union and the United States, which lasted from 1957 – when the Soviets launched the first spacecraft, *Sputnik 1* – to 1969, when the Americans landed on the moon. Before leaving, the astronauts planted an American flag on the moon.

But some people believe that all this was just a big fib.

Doubters say the Americans, desperate to beat the Soviet Union, faked the moon landing. They claim that Armstrong, Aldrin and Collins acted out their mission on a secret film.

And what do they say is the proof? It's all in the flag.

Film of Aldrin planting the American flag on the moon shows it waving, which is impossible since there's no wind on the moon. But the flag wasn't really flapping. When Aldrin planted the flag pole he twisted it, causing the flag to look like it had moved. Some people still aren't convinced, though.

So why don't we just point one of our big space telescopes up the moon to prove it? If we spot the

American flag, we'll know NASA was telling the truth . . .

The resolving power of a telescope – the size of the smallest object it can see at a given distance – is inversely proportional to the diameter of its lens. In other words, to see something small a long way off you need a very big telescope.

A flag is a very small thing, but the *Apollo 11* mission also left its Eagle Lunar Module on the moon. This measures about 4.3 metres across. To see it from Earth, when our planet is at its closest to the moon, would require a telescope with a diameter of nearly 60 metres. The largest telescope now in existence, the Gran Telescopio Canarias on the Spanish island of La Palma, has a diameter of 10.4 metres.

Larger telescopes would be very expensive. It is estimated that the largest telescope currently planned, the (European) Extremely Large Telescope, with a diameter, or aperture, of 39 metres, will cost about £1 billion.

So, we can see distant galaxies through our telescopes, but we cannot see the much closer objects left on the moon because galaxies and galaxy clusters are a bigger target. Galaxies are also bright, making them stand out against the blackness of space, whereas if we wanted to look for Neil Armstrong's moon footprints, which are simply impressions left on the lunar surface, there's barely any contrast at all.

Imagine two walkers about half a metre apart. In your mind's eye, draw lines from your eye to each of the two figures. As the people walk away, they look smaller and closer together and so the angle between the two lines gets smaller.

Eventually, they get so close, and the two focal lines get so close to each other, that the angle becomes tiny and it is impossible to tell the people apart. The smallest angle at which you can still see that they are two people is a measure of the resolving power of an optical instrument, in this case your eye.

We use telescopes because they have a greater resolving power, so they can distinguish between faraway objects. With the naked eye – whose pupil has an aperture of about 2 millimetres – the two ramblers would blur into one object at a distance of about 2 kilometres, assuming perfect eyesight.

The aperture of the Gran Telescopio Canarias on La Palma is about 10 metres, giving it about 5,000 times the resolving power of the naked eye. A telescope of this power would be able to resolve our two ramblers even if they were 10,000 km away. However, the moon is 380,000 km away, and at this distance the telescope has no chance of separating the walkers, let alone their footprints.

If the Hubble Space Telescope, which has been travelling around taking pictures of space since 1990, were brought to within 40 km of the lunar surface it could achieve a resolution of 1 centimetre and make out footprints. Moon-orbiting telescopes have come this close but their optics are not as good.

But even if we *could* just point our super-powerful telescopes in the direction of the moon, would that even convince the sceptics?

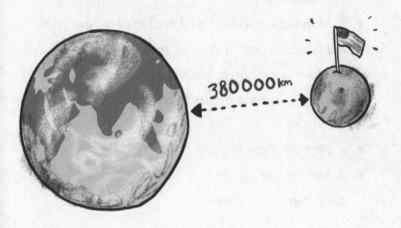

380000 km

HOW TO MEASURE THE SPEED OF SOUND

This experiment is a bit low-tech compared with the 'hot chocolate' experiment used to measure the speed of light. You'll also need access to a very large space . . .

What do I need?

* a hammer
* a grown-up helper capable of safely wielding the hammer
* a hammer-resistant and preferably resonant surface (a wall, piece of metal or rock will do)
* a stopwatch (or a clock with a second hand)
* a very long measuring tape or a measured ball of string
* a pair of binoculars
* a very large garden or flat open space such as a beach or a park

(Add a metal coat hanger, some string and a spoon to check out further properties of sound.)

What do I do?

It goes without saying that this job must be carried out by an adult because a hammer is used.

Ask your helper to begin striking the hard object once every second with the hammer – they'll need

to use the stopwatch and maintain a regular
beat. Begin walking away from your helper,
looking back from time to time. When you are a
few hundred metres apart, use the binoculars if
necessary.

What will I see?

As the distance between you and your helper
increases, the delay between them striking the
hard object and the sound reaching your ears will
become greater. Eventually, the delay will match
the time between each beat and the sound will
once more appear to coincide with the action of
the hammer.

What's going on?

Sound has a relatively low speed through air,
which means you can measure it if you have an
open space large enough. Sound travels at 344 m
per second in dry air at 20 °C. This may vary at
different temperatures, but not by much, so this
experiment works pretty well just about
anywhere.

When the sound of the hammer once again coincides with the 1-second beat, you are ready to measure the speed of sound. Stop walking away at this point and measure the distance between you and the helper. You should be 344 m away, or very close to that.

Of course, very few of us have such long gardens, and finding a flat, open space of that length, unless you live near a beach, may prove troublesome. Then there will be the problem of outside noises interfering with you detecting the beat of the hammer. If this is the case, ask your helper to increase the frequency of the beats to once every half second (in which case you should find yourself about 172 m from your helper when the beats again coincide with the sound), or once every quarter second if they can (when you'll be about 86 m away).

If the sun switched off, how long would it take for us all to freeze to death?

A quick calculation suggests the whole Earth might freeze solid within 45 days.

This is because, without the heat of the sun warming it up, the Earth would radiate away its thermal energy. Most of the energy that Earth captures from the sun is stored in the oceans, which have an average temperature of 15 °C down to a depth of 35 metres. (Energy carried by water at greater depths doesn't count because it would rapidly become isolated from the surface by sheets of floating ice.)

The land would freeze much more quickly than the oceans. Air over the oceans – which would be warmer than the land – would rise, pulling in cold air from the continents. Having cold air above the ocean would cool the surface waters and might increase the circulation of water, because warmer waters rise and colder waters sink, exposing more of the water to the chilling, perpetual night.

How do we know this?

In 1815, a volcano called Mount Tambora, on the Indonesian island of Sumbawa, erupted. It was the largest eruption for 10,000 years and the effects on the environment were huge. There was so much volcanic dust thrown up by the eruption that the dust blocked out the sun! This had a cooling effect on the temperature. It also reduced the ability of the sun's heat to escape from the Earth – a greenhouse effect – which had a heating effect.

The impact of the volcanic eruption was so huge that the next year, 1816, was known as 'the year without summer'. Sunlight dimmed by 25 per cent for a while, leading to a dip in global temperatures of 0.7 °C. That doesn't sound much, but there were huge food shortages as a result of the eruption, and many thousands of people starved.

However, the fall in temperature was actually quite small considering such a big reduction in sunlight. This suggests that the Earth might take longer to freeze than 45 days. Freezing may well be delayed further by the natural greenhouse effect that comes with our atmosphere and the unchanging thermal conditions of our oceans.

But don't panic: the sun can't be turned off like a light bulb.

The reason the sun glows is because its surface is about 5,500 °C and is heated by the nuclear fusion inside its core, which is even hotter – about 15,000,000 °C. Even if fusion in the core could be switched off suddenly, the sun would continue to radiate light just like when you turn off an electric hob in your kitchen and it stays hot for a long time afterwards.

Obviously, the sun is bigger and hotter than anything in your kitchen, so it would continue to radiate heat and light for an even longer time. In fact, the energy produced in the core of the sun takes a really long time to work its way out – millions of years.

So what would happen?

The sun would cool a tiny bit each year. As it cooled, it would contract, releasing gravitational energy that would heat it and offset some of the cooling. That's how stars known as white dwarfs continue shining.

So it would take many millions of years before our descendants even noticed that the sun had switched off. And thankfully, switching off the sun is an experiment the Earth will not undergo for another 5 billion years.

HOW TO MAKE AN EXPLOSION FROM SWEETS AND A FIZZY DRINK

What causes the extraordinarily explosive reaction when Mentos sweets are mixed with cola or another fizzy drink?

Many people are aware of this incredible reaction thanks to viewing the astounding results on the internet. It's a truly awesome sight and one that we simply couldn't leave out . . . so, stand back and prepare to be amazed.

A word of warning: you <u>must</u> get your parent or guardian's permission for this one. It can cause a lot of mess and can be dangerous. And you <u>definitely</u> need to do this outside!

What do I need?

* a large open space
* a tube of Mentos mints
* a 2-litre bottle of cola or other fizzy drink
  (preferably of the diet variety as they usually
  produce a bigger reaction)
* a grown-up

What do I do?

Open the bottle of cola, making sure it is in an
open space and well positioned so that it will not
fall over. Then, open the pack of Mentos and
make sure they are all dropped into the cola at
exactly the same time.

This isn't easy – so it's probably best to get
your grown-up to do this bit. One strategy is to
roll a tube of paper so that it holds all the
Mentos vertically and fit the paper tube into the
bottle neck and release them all at once;
another is to place all the Mentos in a test tube
or similar slim vessel, cover the neck with paper,
tip the test tube upside-down over the open neck

of the bottle and pull the paper away so the
Mentos all fall at once.

Whatever method you adopt, you'll have to be able
to run quickly . . .

What will I see?
A volcanic eruption of cola squirting vertically out
of the bottle. Some reports have recorded a
frothy blast of 6 m in height!

What's going on?
There is still some debate as to what exactly
causes this reaction.

Cola is made from – at the most basic level –
phosphoric acid, sugar, water and carbon dioxide
held in suspension. The initial theory was that the
gum arabic and gelatin in Mentos break down the
surface tension in the cola, which normally
constrains any bubbles, allowing the carbon
dioxide in suspension in the drink to expand into
huge gaseous bubbles and escape very quickly.

Other items dropped into cola – from coins to sugar – also cause it to foam, so while gum arabic may play a role there are almost certainly other factors. What is not in doubt is that the huge amount of gas created causes a massive increase in pressure inside the bottle, spraying the liquid out in an incredible soda eruption.

However, many scientists now think that the reaction is a physical one, rather than a chemical one.

Mentos themselves are covered in tiny pits, which act as nucleation sites for bubbles to form. Not only that, but Mentos sink, passing through a lot of cola very quickly and allowing pressure to build dramatically.

Where do astronauts put their dirty underwear?

One of space travel's most pressing but least-known problems is what to do with dirty underwear.

One solution, attempted by Russian scientists in 1998, was to design a cocktail of bacteria to digest astronauts' cotton and paper underpants. They had hoped that the resulting methane gas (yep, the stuff in farts) could be used to power spacecraft.

The disposal unit would be able to process plastic, cellulose and other organic waste aboard a spacecraft. Cosmonauts identified waste as one of the biggest problems they faced. Each astronaut produces an average of 2.5 kilograms of uncompressed waste a day. To keep waste to a minimum, they have to wear underwear for up to a week (yuck!).

Unfortunately, even though researchers are working on various methods including coating underpants in a solution that will kill any microbes, the problem still hasn't been solved. Underpants are put into waste modules and when these are sent back to Earth the whole module burns up on re-entry to the atmosphere.

. . . and where does astronaut wee go . . ?

Ever since 1961, when astronaut Alan Shepard was waiting to pilot the first US human space flight, and he had to pee his pants on the launchpad – he had to wait there for 5 hours! – there has been the problem of what astronauts do about toilet breaks.

Fortunately, Shepard was wearing cotton underwear, which soaked it up immediately. 'I was totally dry by the time we launched,' he said afterwards.

After that, mission planners started to give the matter more thought.

Today, when astronauts aren't going to be able to get to a toilet (when they are on spacewalks and during launch and landings), they wear Maximum Absorbency Garments, rather like adult nappies, to soak up any wee.

Fortunately, engineers have developed toilets for spaceships and space stations, but they don't always work perfectly. The Russian Mir space station revealed some of the dangers of venting human waste into space. Its toilets did exactly that, and by 2001, when it was retired, the station's solar panels had lost about 40 per cent of their effectiveness, partly because they had been damaged by frozen urine floating in space. Oops!

In 2008, NASA had a very strange idea about what to do with the crew's urine . . . a water-recycling device designed to process the crew's urine for communal consumption. Yes, that's right, the astronauts were going to drink wee . . .

'We can't be delivering water all the time for six

crew,' said space station flight director Ron Spencer. 'Recycling is a must.'

Now they manage to recycle about 80 per cent of the water from the crew's urine. The wastewater is processed using an extensive series of purification techniques, including distillation – which is somewhat tricky in microgravity – filtration, oxidation and ionisation. The final step was the addition of iodine to control microbial growth. The device was intended to process a full day's worth of wastewater in less than 24 hours. 'Today's drinking water was yesterday's waste,' said NASA's Bob Bagdigian, the system's lead engineer.

'We did blind taste tests of the water,' he said. 'Nobody had any strong objections. Other than a faint taste of iodine, it is just as refreshing as any other kind of water. I've got some in my fridge. It tastes fine to me.'

. . . and their poo?

From the outside, the 1972 space shuttle toilet looked much like the uncomfortable apparatus found in the jet airliners of the era. Inside, however, liquid and solid wastes were directed into separate pipes by high-velocity air streams that compensated for the lack of gravity on board the shuttle. The waste was held in two tanks – solids being vacuum-dried, sterilised and deodorised, ready to be pumped out when the shuttle returned to Earth. Depositing the poo in orbit would have obscured rearward vision and possibly interfered with external equipment!

The space shuttle has long since retired, but SpaceX's *Crew Dragon* spaceship and Boeing's *CST-110 Starliner* are set to begin flight tests in 2019, with the aim of taking astronauts to the International Space Station. Both should have toilets.

Today, up on the space station, astronauts have a little plate-sized toilet hole. Their poo is sucked away by a fan. Another funnel sucks their wee away. The poo is stored in a plastic bag, and eventually gets put into the same cargo ship as the underpants, and it all burns up when the module re-enters Earth's atmosphere.

There are some strange ideas about what to do with poo on longer missions, like going to Mars, when long-term exposure to cosmic rays could harm astronauts. Some scientists have proposed using poo to line the walls of the spacecraft and act as a radiation shield against the rays. We're not so sure about that interior design choice!

HOW TO IMPROVE YOUR EYESIGHT

This is one for glasses-wearers, but if you have perfect vision, you can test it on a friend or an adult with spectacles.

If you peer through a small gap, such as that formed between curled-up fingers, objects that were blurred become clearer. The effect is particularly marked if you are short-sighted and remove your glasses or lenses before you try this out.

What do I need?

* the human eye (preferably a short-sighted one)
* a piece of card
* a pin
* paper with words written on it, much like an optician's eye-testing chart
* a comb

What do I do?

Punch a tiny hole in the card with the pin. Fasten your home-made eye-testing card to a wall at a distance where you find it difficult to read. Peer through the pinhole in the card with one eye while keeping the other eye closed.

What will I see?

The writing on the card will become clearer when you look at it through the pinhole. You'll notice the same when you look at other objects around you and in the distance. The effect is particularly noticeable if you are short-sighted (and aren't wearing your glasses). If you have excellent vision, the effect will not be as obvious.

What's going on?

When light enters the eye, it is bent by the lens at the front so it hits the retina at the back of the eye. This allows your brain to create a picture of what you can see. Under normal circumstances, light rays entering the lens are not focused in one place because light is coming from all directions. For you to see a clear image, your eyes have to concentrate all the rays into a single point on the retina.

If your eye is not perfectly shaped, as happens in people with short-sightedness, the outermost rays entering the eye are not bent by the lens enough for them to be focused on the correct point at the back of the eye. The innermost rays entering the eye do not need to be bent as much to hit the middle of the retina and these travel a relatively straight route to form a clear image, even in people who are short-sighted.

However, the outermost rays confuse and blur this image. By looking through a pinhole, the bundle of rays entering your eye is greatly reduced, because the hole allows through only the inner rays that pass through the central portion of your lens straight to your retina. It excludes the peripheral rays that cause the blurring. This means you see images clearly again.

The drawback is that the total amount of light entering your eye is hugely reduced by the pinhole, so images seem darker.

Another thing you can try is using the gaps between the teeth of a comb to reproduce this effect. Native Alaskans have historically worn glasses with narrow slits in them, reproducing the effect of looking through a comb. More importantly, because snow and ice reflect a lot of light, looking through slitted glasses helps to reduce the amount of light entering the eye, aiding vision and preventing snow-blindness.

The accidental aeronauts

Henry Coxwell was one of Victorian England's most famous balloonists. When he agreed to take a scientist high above the Earth, he hadn't banked on taking one of the country's most distinguished meteorologists.

It was 1862, and James Glaisher had been superintendent of the Magnetical and Meteorological Department at Greenwich Royal Observatory for more than twenty years.

He was middle-aged, meticulous and methodical, a man who made measurements, organised observers and sat on important committees. He doesn't sound like a man suited to aeronautical adventures.

But James Glaisher was not after adventure. To him, a balloon was a way of extending his observations into the upper reaches of the atmosphere. In fact, Glaisher hadn't even planned to be the one in the balloon. Glaisher was a member of the balloon committee of the British Association for the Advancement of Science (BA). He'd been planning a balloon trip for years, but no one had a big enough balloon.

Then, in 1861, Henry Coxwell offered to build a balloon big enough for the BA.

The BA jumped at the offer and so Coxwell built a monster balloon, which he named 'Mammoth'. Finding the right observer to fly in it proved harder, though. No one met Glaisher's high standards — so in the end he volunteered himself.

On 17 July 1862, Glaisher discovered what he had let himself in for. The 'Mammoth' was to take off from the gasworks at Wolverhampton in the English Midlands. The windy weather at first made it difficult to inflate the balloon, and then a gust whisked it up before Glaisher had fixed his delicate instruments into position.

A few minutes later, 'Mammoth' emerged above the clouds into brilliant sunshine and Glaisher managed to settle down to work. Coxwell's job was to take the balloon as high as possible. Glaisher's was to record the temperature, air pressure and moisture, make notes on cloud formations and measure the speed and direction of any air currents they encountered — and to check the reliability of the new-fangled aneroid barometer.

By the time they reached 6,000 metres, the men's lips had turned blue and they could hear the pounding of each other's hearts. At 7,500 metres they found breathing difficult. By 9,000 metres, he had made an important discovery. Measurements made on mountains suggested that the temperature dropped uniformly with altitude, around 0.5 °C for every 100 metres. On this ascent, though, the drop was anything but uniform: first the temperature plummeted, then it fell more slowly, then quite unexpectedly rose before dropping sharply again.

By now Coxwell feared the balloon was about to head out to sea and he brought it down, landing with a crash that broke Glaisher's instruments. The meteorologist, however, had proved as heroic as any aeronaut.

Over the next three years, Glaisher made 27 flights. Not all were high-altitude ascents organised by the BA, some were for people willing to pay for a balloon ride over the city.

Summer daytime flights left big gaps in his data, so Glaisher also risked ascents at night and in winter. Whatever the time, every flight was dangerous: he survived several crash landings, had a close shave with a cathedral spire, and more than once faced the prospect of ending up in the sea. But it was one particular flight – on 5 September 1862 – that turned Glaisher and Coxwell into celebrities.

On that day, they took off from Wolverhampton just after 1 o'clock. The balloon rose through a thick bank of cloud, then emerged into bright sunlight. The balloon was rising extremely fast and spinning as it went. They reached an altitude of 8,000 m in 47 minutes.

Then, as the balloon rose higher, Glaisher found it hard to read his thermometer and asked Coxwell for help – only to find him gone. During their giddy ascent, the valve line that allowed Coxwell to control the gas in the balloon had become tangled, so he had climbed up into the hoop above the basket to free it. They continued to rise. At 11,000 metres, Glaisher realised he couldn't move his arms or legs. His head fell sideways. He couldn't speak. Coxwell's hands had frozen to the metal hoop. The only thing he could do was grab the valve line in his teeth, and by nodding his head release some gas. The balloon began to descend. They had, Glaisher reckoned, reached the limit of human existence.

In 1869, Glaisher made a further 28 ascents. His balloon exploits proved fruitful. He refuted the idea that temperature dropped steadily with altitude, and discovered that the atmosphere was like the sea, with currents moving at different speeds and in different directions, some warm and some cold. He found that conditions varied with time of day and season. And he proved aneroid barometers were reliable.

He also learned from experience that England was probably the worst place in the world to do science in a balloon. No matter where you started from, all too soon you were at risk of floating out to sea.

GROSSOLOGY

WELCOME TO THE world of yuck, or what the academic world calls *grossology*. But what we are delighted to discover is that grossology is a genuine scientific field practised by its leading proponent and inventor, Sylvia Branzei, who gave birth to the discipline in 1993 in order to get children more interested in biology and chemistry.

But what exactly qualifies a subject to fall into the grossology category? To be honest, it seems to be everything that kids find funny. A lot of them we've already encountered in previous chapters. Farts are a very important component of the discipline. As is urine. And poo. Which reminds us of an old joke . . .

Five-year-old Alice walked into the kitchen one morning as her biologist father was reading the newspaper. 'Where does poo come from?' she asked.

Startled, he regarded her for a moment before replying. 'Well,' he began. 'You know we've just had breakfast?'

'Yes,' she replied.

He went on: 'The food goes into our tummies and our bodies take out all the good stuff and whatever's left comes out of our bottoms when we go to the toilet, and that's poo.'

She was silent as she digested the enormity of what he'd divulged. 'And Tigger?'

Why do we have to both poo and wee?

Ever wondered why your body can't just get rid of everything it needs in one way, rather than both poo and wee?

The process of 'excretion' is the passing of material from inside our bodies to the outside. Our kidneys excrete urine, our skin excretes sweat, our lungs excrete water and carbon dioxide, and the inside of our bowel tube excretes many things along its length to assist digestion, as well as disposing of waste products in our bile. The other excreta our bodies produce include tears, earwax, and various secretions associated with our reproductive processes. Spots too are caused by excretions that have gone awry.

Poo, on the other hand, consists of undigested food and bacteria, plus bile from the liver, which gives excrement its brown colour. It has been through our body, but it has stayed within our digestive system and never actually got inside our cells and blood. Only the bits that are digested get properly inside us.

Urine, for example, is the result of the kidneys filtering waste products that are carried around in our blood. When our cells break down molecules called nucleic acids and proteins, this produces waste compounds such as urea. Furthermore, urine also contains water and dissolved compounds from the blood, because sometimes these need to be excreted to maintain the right concentrations of water and useful compounds inside and outside our cells.

The fact we have two systems for getting rid of waste is fairly obvious, because we have a separate opening for each: the anus and the urethra. In other organisms, the distinction between the systems isn't as obvious. Animals such as birds, reptiles and amphibians possess a cloaca, which serves as a common opening for both liquid and solid wastes. Insects blur the line even further:

rather than having a distinct urinary system, they
relyonMalpighian tubules in their digestive
systems – outgrowths of
the gut that
perform the
same
filtration
function as
our kidneys.

HOW TO CHANGE THE COLOUR
OF YOUR WEE WITH DIFFERENT DRINKS

What do I need?
* a variety of drinks of different colours: cola,
  water, cranberry or orange juice, or anything
  else with an interesting hue that you can
  think of

* a human digestive and urinary system
* a toilet

What do I do?

Sample the drinks in turn after an initial visit to the toilet to ensure that the next visit's urine will contain mainly the products of your most recent drink. You may have to do this over a period of days in order to establish a rhythm, perhaps consuming each drink at the same time on consecutive days. Make sure that you don't have anything else to drink between consuming each liquid and visiting the toilet. Note the colour of your urine after each drink.

What will I see?

You may notice variations in the yellow colour of your urine, but you will not, under normal circumstances, notice any colouring from the original drink showing through.

What's going on?

Coloured substances in drinks (or food) are usually organic compounds that the human body has an amazing ability to metabolise, breaking them down into colourless carbon dioxide, water and urea. The toughest stuff is taken care of by the liver, which is a veritable living waste incinerator, while the kidneys take care of removing waste products from your blood. By the time it leaves your body the liquid is almost unrelated in chemical composition to the original liquid you consumed.

Any substance, solid or liquid, that goes down your oesophagus passes through the digestive tract. As we already revealed, if it isn't absorbed, it becomes poo. Waste produced by the kidneys is added to any excess water you have consumed to produce urine of various shades of yellow. This is stored in and passed out from the bladder.

So any coloured compound that you drink either will or will not interact biochemically with the body's systems. If it does, this interaction will eliminate its colour. If it does not, the digestive system will usually decline to absorb it and it will be excreted in the faeces, which, you will have noticed, show considerably more variation in colour than urine.

Some coloured substances can make it through your digestive system and into your urine. This occurs when the intake of coloured substances exceeds what the body can quickly metabolise and the colouring is not removed as the liquid leaves the body. If you want to see this effect you should consume a large quantity of beetroot soup. You'll notice that your urine takes on a distinctly pinkish hue.

My dad keeps telling me not to pick my nose and eat it. Will eating my bogeys do me any harm?

Picking and eating are for cherries. Even if eating your bogeys isn't bad for you, chewing them could affect the health of your friendships!

But if you really want a snot supper, then eating bogeys probably won't do you much harm.

For the most part, any germs they contained would be digestible or would otherwise die in your gut. But this is not always the case: some germs do infect people via the nose, and some toxic dust particles do stick in your phlegm. It is not for nothing that your nose hairs stop bugs and dust

from landing in your lungs or gut. Blowing your
nose would not stop everything, but it is better
than guzzling snot.

How many times do people fart per day?

Here's a piece of trivia with which to impress your
friends: the average adult in the Western world
farts roughly ten times a day, releasing enough gas
to inflate a party balloon.

More than 99 per cent of these emissions are made
up of five odourless gases. What exactly causes
their foul smell has long been a matter of debate.
But in 2001, one man believed he had the answer.

Michael Levitt, a gastroenterologist at the Veterans
Administration Medical Center in Minneapolis, had
been studying farts for over thirty years and solved
numerous mysteries. As a result, he has become
famous and his work has been written about in
newspapers around the world.

Many scientists would welcome this exposure, but for Levitt it was disastrous. Readers would write angry letters to his employers complaining that his research was a waste of money. What went wrong?

Part of the problem was farts are funny. The temptation to turn out stories brimming with puns and fart jokes was often too great for journalists to resist. One even called him Dr Fart.

But Levitt's work was serious. For instance, he was the first to correctly identify the gases that make farts smell. Evaluating a smell is a difficult task, so Levitt turned to the noses of two people with a rather unusual ability. Both could identify different sulphur-containing gases purely by smell. These lucky individuals were asked to evaluate the farts of 16 healthy men and women who, the previous evening, had eaten 200 grams of beans to ensure ample gas production. Levitt said the results pointed to hydrogen sulphide as the culprit in smelly farts, accompanied to a lesser extent by other sulphur-based gases.

Levitt's work was far from pointless – it has saved lives. Hydrogen and methane, two of the main gases that form in the gut, are combustible. In the 1980s, they caused a number of fatal explosions during otherwise routine operations on the gut. Somehow the purgatives used to clean the gut enhanced the production of hydrogen or methane and a chance spark during the operation triggered an explosion. Levitt and others have since developed purgatives that clean the bowel with minimal gas production. Thanks to Dr Fart, gut explosions are now rare.

HOW TO FIND OUT THE TIME IT TAKES FOR TYPES OF FOOD TO TURN INTO POO

The gross factor looms large in this one. And for the really brave, there can be fun with a kebab skewer afterwards! (But do check with your parents first and ask them to supervise you.)

What do I need?

* a human digestive system
* sugar
* streaky bacon
* sweetcorn
* tomato
* mushrooms
* celery
* beetroot
* a stick or kebab skewer for poking through the products

What do I do?

Cook and eat the foodstuffs, plus anything else you fancy — fibre-rich vegetables produce the most interesting results.

What will I see?

Possibly nothing, depending on how closely you are prepared to inspect your poo.

Plant material such as red tomato is often visible in human excrement, as are the skins of peppers. Sweetcorn is probably the most obvious retained product of the human digestive system, its yellow colour standing out particularly well in faeces, although celery and mushrooms are also difficult to break down. Our old friend beetroot — which can do fun things to your urine — can also give your poo a fascinating reddish hue.

What's going on?

Simple sugars such as glucose will be absorbed into the bloodstream relatively quickly and will not appear in any noticeable form after passing through the body. They may even pass directly from the mouth into cheeks and gums because their molecules are small enough to pass directly into human cells.

However, most food needs processing by our digestive system before it will pass into our bloodstream and become useful fuel. The journey begins in our mouth where the food is crushed until the pieces are small enough to swallow, and enzymes begin to break it down further. Once in the stomach, it is attacked by more enzymes and acids in gastric juices and is blended by the churning motion of the muscles in the stomach wall. A couple of hours later, this semi-liquid passes into the small intestine, from where much of it is absorbed into the bloodstream.

Some components, such as dietary fibre, cannot be digested and move on to the large intestine. This takes about six hours. Once there, more water is absorbed by the body so that only the indigestible material remains. This may take up to 36 hours before the remaining waste is expelled in our poo, which is about 75 per cent water.

Of the various foodstuffs we eat, sugar is the first to be absorbed, followed by proteins (from eggs, nuts and non-fatty meat) in about six hours, and finally by various types of fat over longer periods, although the age, health and size of the eater will affect all these timings.

As you will discover from carrying out the experiment, some components of food, such as fibre, are hardly broken down at all and, as in the case of sweetcorn, pass out of the body relatively untouched. The lignins in mushrooms and the cellulose in celery are also relatively unscathed after a journey through your body.

Those brave enough — and you should do this with a grown-up — can take a long kebab skewer and

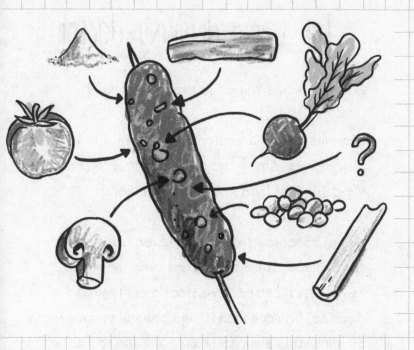

poke through the poo to see what they can recognise. If you do feel up to attempting this, disposable gloves are a sensible precaution, and you should certainly wash your hands thoroughly after disposing of the experimental material.

The vomit-drinking doctor

How far would you go to prove your point?

Stubbins Ffirth, a doctor-in-training living in Philadelphia during the early nineteenth century, went further than most. Way further.

Having observed that yellow fever ran riot during the summer, but disappeared over the winter, Ffirth hypothesised it was not a contagious disease. He reckoned it was caused by an excess of stimulants such as heat, food and noise. To prove his hunch, Ffirth set out to demonstrate that no matter how much he exposed himself to yellow fever, he wouldn't catch it.

He started by making a small incision in his arm and pouring 'fresh black vomit' obtained from a yellow-fever patient into the cut. He didn't get sick.

But he didn't stop there. His experiments grew progressively bolder – and grosser. He made deeper incisions in his arms into which he poured black vomit. He dribbled the stuff in his eyes. He filled a room with heated 'regurgitation vapours' – a vomit sauna – and remained there for two hours, breathing in the air. He experienced a 'great pain in my head, some nausea, and perspired very freely', but was otherwise OK.

Next Ffirth began ingesting the vomit. He fashioned some of the black matter into pills and swallowed them down. He mixed half an ounce of fresh vomit with water and drank it. Finally, he gathered his courage and quaffed pure, undiluted black vomit fresh from a patient's mouth. Still he didn't get sick.

Ffirth rounded out his experiment by liberally smearing himself with other yellow-fever-tainted fluids: blood, saliva, perspiration and urine.

Healthy as ever, he declared his hypothesis proven in his 1804 thesis.

But . . .

He was wrong. Yellow fever is very contagious, but it requires direct transmission into the bloodstream, usually by a mosquito, to cause infection.

Considering the efforts Ffirth took to infect himself, it must be considered something of a miracle he remained alive.

WHY DO BOYS HAVE NIPPLES?

CRAZY EXPERIMENTS AND BONKERS INVENTIONS

NECESSITY IS THE mother of invention, as the old saying goes. While some of the mad inventions and experiments in this chapter aren't exactly what we'd consider necessary, they're certainly entertaining!

Have you ever found yourself running late for school? Next time, why not fling yourself there like a human cannonball? In case of a crash landing, an indestructible lunch might be useful. And don't worry if you forget your lunch – a nice spot of mud could make a nutritious alternative, according to one scientist.

We've got answers to all these pressing questions and more: how do you design an alien? Would you let a vacuum cleaner cut your hair? How do you leave secret messages in the bathroom? And why can't you tickle yourself?

How do you design an alien?

What are the rules of thumb that life forms anywhere in the galaxy would have to follow?

The famous British geneticist Conrad Waddington believed that any higher life form would have to look like . . . er . . . Conrad Waddington.

But most people think that if evolution on Earth was run through again, land vertebrates – and that includes us – would be unlikely to reappear. And if they did we'd look very different. Of course, this applies to other planets too.

So, if we can't have humans on other planets, what can we have?

There are patterns of general problems and common solutions that apply to life anywhere in the universe. We know this because different species on Earth invent identical solutions separately. Birds, bats, insects and some fish all fly. And plants and some bacteria photosynthesise. These universal solutions will be found on any other planets with life.

So we know that life will be formed of universal solutions – such as the elephant's huge legs to support great bulk in gravity – and local or parochial ones – such as its trunk, which developed from a need, on Earth, to pick up food from its feeding spots. Its food on another planet might not have required trunk-to-mouth delivery.

The difficulty, therefore, is in recognising universal solutions – which aliens will possess – and parochial ones – which they will not. Parochials normally happen only once – the trunk – universals more times – flying. So the fact that we have joints seems universal; the number of digits on a limb is not. Eyes, yes. External ears, probably not.

This means the standard clichés of science fiction would not hold up. Little green men that look just like humans is, sadly, illogical. Little green splots are so much more believable.

Is that a furry submarine?

When is a sub not a sub?

The answer, as an embarrassed Swedish navy had to admit in 1996, is when it's a mink or an otter.

What the navy thought was the sinister sound of Soviet propellers was, in fact, the furious paddling of little legs. A scientific commission set up by the government and chaired by the former director of the Swedish Engineering Science Academy, Hans Forsberg, concluded that most of the invading submarines reported by the navy were mythical. Of more than 6,000 reports of 'alien underwater activity' between 1981 and 1994, the commission found firm evidence for only six incidents.

In every other case the evidence, often based on sightings by the public, was unreliable.

On 40 occasions between 1992 and 1994, a defence network of microphones attached to buoys detected the sound of bubbles caused by a rotational movement in the water. The navy estimated the speed at up to 200 revolutions per minute, and assumed it must be submarine propellers. But the navy was wrong. According to the commission's secretary, Ingvar Akesson, tests with swimming mink or otters showed that they could produce the same readings as propellers.

How do you make an indestructible sandwich?

First came the atom bomb, the stealth bomber and the airborne laser. Then in 2002, came one of the US military's most fearsome weapons: the indestructible sandwich.

Capable of surviving airdrops, rough handling and extreme climates, and just about anything except a soldier's jaws, the pocket sandwich was designed to stay 'fresh' for up to three years at 26 °C (about the temperature of a warm summer's day), or for six months at 38 °C (just over body temperature).

For years, the US army had wanted to supplement its standard battlefield rations, called 'Meal, Ready-to-Eat' (MRE), with something that could be eaten on the move. Although MREs already contained ingredients that could be made into sandwiches, these had to be pasteurised and stored in separate pouches, and the soldiers needed to make the sandwiches themselves.

'The water activities of the different sandwich components need to complement each other,' explained Michelle Richardson, project officer at the US Army Soldier Systems Center in Natick, Massachusetts. 'If the water activity of the meat is too high you might get soggy bread.'

To tackle the problem, researchers at Natick used fillings such as pepperoni and chicken, to which they added substances called humectants, which stop water leaking out. The humectants not only prevented water from the fillings soaking into the bread, but also limited the amount of moisture available for bacterial growth. The sandwiches were then sealed, without pasteurisation, in laminated plastic pouches that also included sachets of oxygen-scavenging chemicals. A lack of oxygen helped prevent the growth of yeast, mould and bacteria.

Soldiers who tried the pepperoni and barbecue-chicken pocket sandwiches found them 'acceptable'.

HOW TO MAKE PLASTIC OUT OF MILK AND VINEGAR

You would imagine that you'd need some pretty noxious, smelly chemicals to make plastic, but you can actually find the things you need to make malleable, doughy pieces of material in your own home.

Instead of putting vinegar on your fish and chips and wasting your milk in your tea, use the two liquids to become a polymer chemist . . .

What do I need?
* a pint of milk
* a saucepan
* a sieve
* a spoon for stirring
* 20 ml of white vinegar
* rubber gloves

* water

* a grown-up helper

What do I do?

Pour the milk into the pan and gently warm it.
When the milk is simmering (don't let it boil) stir
in the white vinegar until you notice whitish-yellow
rubbery lumps beginning to curdle in the mixture
at the same time as the liquid clears. Turn off
the heat and let the pan cool.

What will I see?

First of all, you'll smell the vinegary reaction,
which is the key to this process at work. As the
vinegar is added and stirred, the liquid gets
clearer and the yellowy rubbery lumps form.

When the pan has cooled, you can sieve the
lumps from the liquid, tipping the liquid down the
sink. Put on the rubber gloves and wash the
lumps in water. You can then press them
together into one big blob — they will be squishy

and will feel as if they are going to fall apart, but they will stick together after some firm kneading.

You can now use your artistic skills to fashion the material into the shapes of your choice – *New Scientist* staff came up with balls, stars, a heart-shape for a pendant and even dinosaur footprints. Leave the material to dry for a day or two and it will be hard and plastic enough to paint and varnish.

What's going on?

You have used the combination of an acid – in this case vinegar, which contains acetic acid – and heat to precipitate casein (a protein) from the milk.

Casein is not soluble in an acid environment and so, when the vinegar is added, it appears in the form of globular plastic-like lumps. Casein behaves like the plastics that we see in so many objects around us, such as computer keyboards or phones, because it has a similar molecular form. The plastics in everyday objects are based on long-chain molecules called polymers. These are of high molecular weight and get their strength from the way their billions of interwoven criss-crossing molecules tangle together.

PS: Some forms of cheese-making rely on a similar technique – the name casein comes from *caseus*, the Latin for cheese. The Indian cheese known as paneer is made in a very similar way to the plastic you have just made, although in this case lemon juice is the acid used rather than vinegar. Afterwards, unlike our plastic milk, it is not dried out and allowed to harden to tooth-breaking consistency, and so remains soft and edible.

Could we ever eat mud?

In 1957, it was thought that mud dredged up from the bottom of Lake Victoria in Africa, 20 metres down, might be turned into food for pigs and chickens, according to the director of the East African Fisheries Research Organisation (EAFRO), Mr R. S. A. Beauchamp.

After studying the composition of the fauna and flora that are found in Lake Victoria, Beauchamp's colleagues discovered that there was not as much plankton as they had expected in the water, because of a shortage of sulphur. In lakes in temperate climates, millions of dead plankton, weeds and water animals fall to the bottom every year and when they decompose they return to the water the elements they took from it to grow.

But the mud found on the bed of Lake Victoria was very slow to decompose because of lack of oxygen. This meant that at the bottom of the lake, locked up in layers of mud that ran to tens of metres deep, was the accumulated richness of thousands of years' deposits. The water lying above was infertile because of its lack of nutrients.

EAFRO suggested that swamps could be filled up with the rich lake mud to make good land for market gardens, but Beauchamp also believed that, dried and powdered, the mud could become nutritious food for pigs and poultry because it contained numerous valuable minerals and also considerable amounts of protein.

The dried mud was, apparently, not unpleasant to eat – Beauchamp tried it himself and offered it to his friends and family in order to prove his point.

Want to be a human cannonball?

Believe it or not, the old circus trick of firing a person from a cannon was being considered by the US Defense Advanced Research Projects Agency (DARPA) as a way to get special forces, police officers and firefighters on to the roofs of tall buildings in a hurry.

A ramp with side rails would be placed on the ground near the target building at an angle of about 80 degrees. A (very brave) person would then sit in a chair, like a pilot's ejector seat, attached to the ramp. Compressed air from a cylinder underneath would be rapidly released to shoot the chair up the ramp's guide rails. At the top, the chair would come to an instant halt, leaving the person to fly up and over the edge of the roof, to land (one hopes) safely on top of the building.

Of course, the trick would be to get the trajectory just right. But the DARPA patent suggested a computer could automatically devise the correct angle and speed of ascent. It also claimed that a 4-metre-tall launcher could put a man on the top of a 5-storey building in less than 2 seconds.

Most of us would probably prefer the stairs . . .

Could toothpaste save your life?

In 1967, from the research laboratories of American industry there came a toothpaste that glowed in the dark and reflected the headlights of motor cars.

It was the first toothpaste that could be advertised as making a definite contribution to road safety – as long as those who used it remembered to walk facing the traffic and to keep grinning!

What do you wear to save yourself from bear attacks?

In December 2001, a Canadian man and a 3-metre, 585-kilogram Kodiak bear were set to face off. It was an attempt to test a handmade bear-proof suit.

The suit and its maker, Troy Hurtubise of North Bay, Ontario, won a 1998 Ig Nobel prize – awarded annually for improbable research projects – and an entry in the 2002 Guinness Book of World Records for the most expensive research suit ever constructed. Fifteen years of tinkering and US$100,000 went into the design, which incorporated plastic, rubber, chainmail, galvanised steel, titanium – and thousands of metres of duct tape.

The suit proved itself to be virtually indestructible. It survived two strikes with a 136-kilogram tree trunk, 18 collisions with a 3-tonne truck at 50 kilometres an hour, and numerous strikes by arrows, bullets, axes and baseball bats. 'I've never had a bruise,' said Hurtubise.

But the suit had never come up against the very thing it was meant to protect against – a grizzly bear. On 9 December 2001, in an undisclosed location in western Canada, all that changed. In a 'controlled attack', the Kodiak, a larger, heavier subspecies of the grizzly, was to put it to the test.

The bear, which appeared on TV commercials and in movies, was to be instructed by its handler to attack for ten seconds. Showbiz aside, Hurtubise stressed that it was a real bear. 'Real teeth, real claws, real power,' he said.

Hurtubise was banking on the titanium layers around the chest, head and lower body to protect him. 'If there's a weakness,' he said, 'it would be the chainmail joints.' Hurtubise said he was excited, but a little anxious too. 'Little things like trucks and baseball bats and axes and things – you don't feel that,' he said. 'This is a bear.'

So what happened?

The first live tests of Troy Hurtubise's grizzly-proof suit found that its best protective feature was its bizarre appearance. Hurtubise put on the suit and squared up to a 145-kilogram female grizzly but the bear just found it too weird. When confronted by Hurtubise in the Ursus Mark VI suit, the bear smelled a human, but saw an alien. 'There's no grizzly that's going to come near you in that suit,' the bear handler told him, after he spent ten minutes in a cage with the cowering animal.

In an earlier test, the suit had to go it alone, without Hurtubise inside, with a fearsome opponent – a 545-kilogram male Kodiak. The suit was placed into the cage of the giant bear, to get him accustomed to it. Eventually, the bear began to sniff the contraption, and then proceeded to jump on it.

Though it ripped off chunks of rubber, all was well until the bear began to shred the protective chainmail and was called off by the handler. Hurtubise learned that you should never skimp on chainmail.

Without effective chainmail, the bear handler decided not to allow an attack with Hurtubise inside the suit. But he did permit Hurtubise to take on the smaller female grizzly, although no contact was allowed. It took the bear a while to approach but soon enough it was just six inches away. 'I could feel her breath coming through my visor,' said Hurtubise. 'I was terrified.'

As far as we know, Hurtubise never made it back into the cage with another grizzly. He reportedly sold the bear suit and invested the money in designing indestructible suits for soldiers and a device that allows humans to see through solid objects. He later went bankrupt.

Why do we laugh when we're tickled?

Tickling is a serious business.

In 1933, Clarence Leuba, a professor of psychology from Ohio, made his home the setting for an ambitious experiment. He planned to find out whether laughter is a learned response to being tickled or one that we are born with.

To achieve this goal, he determined never to allow his newborn son to associate laughter with tickling. This meant that no one – in particular his wife – was allowed to laugh in the presence of the child while tickling or being tickled. Leuba planned to observe whether his son eventually laughed when tickled or grew up dismissing wiggling fingers in his armpits with a stony silence.

The Leuba household became a tickle-free zone, except during experimental sessions in which Leuba subjected his son to laughter-free tickling.

During these sessions, Leuba followed a strict procedure. First he put on a 30-centimetre by 40-centimetre cardboard mask, maintaining a 'smileless, sober expression' behind it. Then he tickled his son in a pre-determined pattern – first light, then vigorous – in order of armpits, ribs, chin, neck, knees, then feet.

Everything went well until 23 April 1933, when Leuba's wife had made a confession. On one occasion, after her son's bath, she had 'bounced him up and down while laughing and saying, 'Bouncy, Bouncy'. It is not clear if this was enough to ruin the experiment. What is clear is that by month seven, Leuba's son was happily screaming with laughter when tickled.

Undeterred, Leuba repeated the experiment after his daughter was born in February 1936. He obtained the same result. By the age of seven months, his daughter was laughing when tickled. Leuba concluded that laughter must be a response to being tickled that we are all born with.

Why can't you tickle yourself?

In the early 1970s, psychologists from both Oxford and Sheffield tried to find out just why tickling yourself isn't funny. What they found out wasn't quite as simple as you might expect.

Charles Darwin, the naturalist who came up with the theory of evolution, was intrigued by the ineffectiveness of the self-administered tickle. His interest, though, was mainly in the biological value of ticklishness and laughter. The scientists in this study, on the other hand, wanted to find out what was involved in tickling. To do this, they lined up 30 volunteers brave enough to be tickled by some special tickle apparatus.

Three types of tickle were administered: the first by an experimenter; the second a self-tickle where the volunteers moved the handle of the tickle apparatus themselves; the third by an experimenter, but with the volunteer's hand on the handle. The idea of this last method was to see if there was any effect on the ticklishness when the subject went through the motion of tickling but was not actually in command.

Unsurprisingly, tickling was most effective when done by someone else, and least effective when the volunteers tickled themselves. Someone else tickling you with your own arms was in between.

So why was this the case? When the volunteer was tickled using his or her own hand the tickling was less effective, but it still tickled a bit . . .

Studies since have revealed that when we move our arms (or legs), the brain region known as the cerebellum predicts what the tickling movement will be and sends a signal to another part of the brain – the part of the brain that processes the feelings of touch – essentially telling it to calm down. Because the brain knows the tickle is coming, it stops it tickling.

HOW TO LEAVE SECRET MESSAGES IN YOUR BATHROOM

What do I need?

* a bathroom that readily steams up
* a mirror
* a finger

What do I do?

Wait until you are taking a hot bath or shower (*New Scientist* is very green – there's no excuse for water wastage or excess heating) and your bathroom has steamed up, then draw or write on your mirror with your finger. After you've finished bathing, open the windows and let the room cool. The next time you or a family member takes a bath and the room steams up, look at the mirror.

What will I see?

Your original message or picture, which vanished when the room cooled down and the condensation on the mirror evaporated, will return when the bathroom steams up and the mirror mists over.

What's going on?

When water vapour condenses on a dry mirror, it does so as separate droplets – a process known as 'dropwise condensation'. These droplets effectively screen the mirror so that it appears opaque.

When you draw on the surface with your finger, the droplets come together to form a thin film of transparent water, so the mirror becomes reflective again in these areas – this has a fancy name: it's called 'filmwise condensation'. When the mirror warms up, or the air humidity falls, the droplets evaporate and the image disappears because the surrounding droplets no longer contrast with it.

However, the film of water evaporates more slowly than the droplets because of its lower surface area. If it does not have time to evaporate completely before the bathroom steams up again, any condensation occurring soon afterwards will be dropwise where there were droplets before, and filmwise where some of the film remains. The image will then reappear on the glass.

However, this only explains how mirror drawings return in the short term. If the mirror dries completely, the pattern should not normally reappear when further condensation occurs. But this presumes that your drawing finger is entirely clean, which is unlikely.

When you draw an image in the condensation, your finger will almost certainly leave behind traces of grease or sweat, plus possibly shampoo or soap. These traces are transparent, so when the condensation disappears you can't see them. The next time water vapour condenses on the mirror, however, there is a noticeable difference in droplet size between those forming on the clean glass and those forming on the greasy or soap-contaminated glass.

Grease will tend to repel water droplets, while water-loving surfactants such as soap will reduce the droplet size and generate a smoother, clear film of water. Whatever the cause, as the mirror steams up again, the image you drew will contrast with the opaque mist on the surrounding glass.

Would you let your vacuum cleaner cut your hair?

In the mid-1980s, a South African designer called Jan Louw came up with an attachment for a vacuum cleaner that let people cut their own hair.

The cutter looked like a hair dryer but was connected to the hose of your vacuum cleaner. The air sucked in through the open end of the 'hair dryer' nozzle would drive a turbine, which rotated one blade over another stationary blade to mimic the action of scissors. The user would slide the end of the nozzle over the scalp and hair would be sucked in to be sliced by the blades. The shorter the nozzle length, the shorter the haircut. Cut hair ended up in the bag of the vacuum cleaner.

Can your pencils do this?

At 5.30 p.m., Fred Tee picked up the folder with his papers in, put on his trilby and headed for home. Like most of the workforce at the Cumberland Pencil Company, he lived just a few minutes' walk from the factory in Keswick.

As soon as it grew dark, Tee, who was the factory's technical manager, set off back to the works and quietly let himself into his laboratory through the back door. This was the fifth night in a row that he and his fellow managers had met after work.

It was 1942, and Britain was at war. Tee and his colleagues had been asked to produce a special type of pencil: it must have a secret compartment just large enough to hold a tightly rolled map and a tiny compass. Only the managers were in on the secret, sworn to silence by the Official Secrets Act.

Tee and the Cumberland Pencil Company had been commissioned by a mysterious man from London who claimed to be a civil servant from the Ministry of Supply's Clothing and Textile Department. His name was Charles Fraser-Smith and his real job was to supply equipment and gadgets for MI6, MI9 (part of the War Office) and the Special Operations Executive. He was after everything from miniature cameras to surgical saws, edible notepaper to forged foreign currency. He was always on the lookout for new and unusual ways to hide equipment that would help downed airmen avoid capture, prisoners of war escape, and secret agents get their information safely back to Britain. He was the original 'Q' immortalised in the James Bond movies.

Fraser-Smith was bombarded with requests for devices with secret compartments, and conjured up shaving brushes, pipes and pens, golf balls and even shoelaces that concealed escape equipment. His strategy was to approach a well-known firm that made a suitable object and ask if they could make a version with some unusual features. Across Britain, designers and engineers took up the challenge.

So when Fraser-Smith needed a pencil with a secret compartment he visited the oldest and best-known manufacturer in the country, the Cumberland Pencil Company. Was it possible, he asked, to make a pencil that would hold a tightly rolled map, about 12 centimetres long, plus a compass – without anyone noticing? A pencil was a standard piece of navigation equipment, making it an ideal place to hide escape gear.

There were six separate operations in producing a pencil – including making the leads, gluing them into grooved cedar-wood slats, shaping the pencils and embossing them with the company name, before packing them into boxes. Although it would have been easier to create the hiding place early in the process, Tee decided that the extra step should be done right at the end to ensure that none of the workforce realised what was going on.

After hours and at weekends, Tee and his fellow managers crept into the factory, took a box of finished pencils off the shelf and carefully drilled out the insides, leaving a short stretch of lead-filled pencil at the working end. The next job was to slide in the map, fix the metal ferrule to the end, slip in a tiny brass compass and glue the rubber back on top. At the end of the job, the pencil looked just as it had at the start.

But where did Fraser-Smith find compasses and maps small enough to fit in a pencil?

No compass existed that was small enough. But in London, Fraser-Smith discovered two brothers who were making large compasses for the navy. He asked them to make something 'smaller than they had ever seen or heard of'. They did, and over the next few years the miniature compasses turned up inside pens and pencils, in battledress buttons, hairbrushes and even in place of fillings in airmen's teeth!

And what about the map? Fraser-Smith toyed with handkerchiefs printed with invisible ink that would emerge when soaked with urine. These were too bulky to hide inside gadgets, so he had to think of something else. The maps in the Cumberland pencils were printed on a fine, non-rustling tissue paper made specially for the job, then rolled around a soft wire that was folded over at the tip to secure the paper. Three cotton ties ensured the map stayed tightly rolled and no more than 3 millimetres in diameter. There were four maps, which were fitted into a series of pencils numbered 101 to 104. Pencils labelled 101 held a general map of Germany. The other three concealed larger-scale maps of different sectors of the country.

So did any downed airmen or prisoners find their way home with the help of a Cumberland pencil?

Fraser-Smith was certain his gadgets saved lives and helped people get home, but there were no official records. Officially, he didn't exist. And Tee and his colleagues would never find out. Their pencils didn't exist either.

Is this how to talk to the animals?

Some animals prick up their ears to get messages across. Karola Baumann of Düsseldorf believed that therefore, we could communicate better with animals if they could see us pricking up our ears.

In 1998, Baumann and her colleagues described a device that they hoped would transform the wearer into Doctor Dolittle. It was a skullcap with two short 'masts' at either side over the ears, each carrying a large replica of an animal's ear. These ears could be moved as the human 'talked' to an animal.

The doctor who experimented on himself

If you want to make it into the history books as a hero of medical science, you can't beat a bit of experimentation – on yourself, that is.

Is a new drug safe? Take some and find out. Does that vaccine work? Try it and see. The only catch is that you have to survive the experiment long enough to write up your results in a suitably eminent medical journal. One man who did, and earned worldwide fame, was the German surgeon August Bier.

In 1898, Bier invented spinal anaesthesia. After a few promising tests on patients, Bier wanted to find out how much they felt during an operation and why they developed horrible headaches afterwards. So, one summer's evening, he asked his assistant to anaesthetise him. It was an experiment they might have preferred forgotten.

The two surgeons had finished work for the day. But instead of going home, Bier and his young assistant, August Hildebrandt, began to prepare for one more operation. What happened next was not so much heroic as comic.

In the 1890s, general anaesthesia was pretty dodgy. Chloroform sent patients gently to sleep – but there was no room for mistakes. A few drops too many and the patient would be dead before the surgeon picked up his scalpel. Ether wasn't quite so dangerous, but it was slow to act and so surgeons sometimes started to operate before their patients had gone under – ouch! The survivors suffered unpleasant side effects, from violent headaches and vomiting to ether pneumonia.

Bier reasoned it should be possible to banish sensation from most of the body without knocking the patient out completely by injecting a small dose of cocaine into the cerebrospinal fluid that bathes the spinal cord. He tried his technique on half a dozen patients. They lost sensation from the lower part of their bodies long enough for him to carve out chunks of diseased bone from their ankles, knees and shins and even the thigh and pelvis.

The procedure was simple enough.
Hildebrandt had to make a lumbar puncture, which is done by plunging a large needle between the bones of the lower back and through the membranes that protect the spinal cord into the fluid-filled space beneath. Then he had to fit a syringe on the needle and inject a solution of cocaine.

Hildebrandt made the lumbar puncture. Then, with his finger over the hub of the needle to prevent fluid from leaking out, he took up the syringe of cocaine – only to find it was the wrong fit. As he fumbled with the needles, Bier's cerebrospinal fluid began to squirt out. Horrified, Hildebrandt stopped and plugged the wound.

This was when the pair should have called it a day. Instead, Hildebrandt offered to take Bier's place.

At 7.38 p.m., after checking the needles more carefully, Bier began. The cocaine worked fast. Within seven minutes, pricking Hildebrandt on the thigh with needles was felt only as pressure and he couldn't feel his feet being tickled. By 13 minutes into the experiment, Bier stubbed out a cigar on Hildebrandt's leg and still nothing.

But how much more could Hildebrandt take? Bier increased his efforts. He smashed a heavy iron hammer into Hildebrandt's shin bone and then, when that failed to have any effect, gave his private parts a sharp tug. Bier then stabbed Hildebrandt in the leg.

After 45 minutes, the effect of the cocaine began to wear off. The two surgeons, one missing a significant amount of cerebro-spinal fluid, the other battered, burnt and suffering from serious stab wounds, went out for dinner.

The next morning, Bier woke feeling bright and breezy. By the afternoon he had turned pale, his pulse was weak and he felt dizzy whenever he stood up. He had to go to bed and he stayed there for the next nine days until he felt better.

Hildebrandt was even sicker. The first night he had a splitting headache and was sick. But with Bier in bed, he still had to go to work.

But as far as Bier was concerned, the experiment was a huge success. He had spinal anaesthesia that was far safer than general anaesthesia, and within two years surgeons around the world were using it. Bier put the headaches down to the loss of cerebrospinal fluid, and he was right – this was finally proved in the 1950s.

Unsurprisingly Hildebrandt had gone right off Bier. When a row blew up over who had really been first to invent spinal anaesthesia, Hildebrandt championed Bier's rival, an American neurologist called James Corning. Hildebrandt never said why. Perhaps he was shocked by the enthusiasm with which Bier had beaten him up . . .

SCIENCE HEADLINES FROM YESTERYEAR

It's hard to believe that inventions like the internet, the mobile phone and a colour television were impossible to imagine a hundred years ago. Just take a look at some of these headlines from history below!

We wonder what future generations will think of our cutting-edge technology in years to come . . .

Remarkable though the 'instant' processes for black-and-white and colour photography appear today, they are by no means the last word in techniques for the amateur. Simultaneous recording of sight and sound on tape is just one of the coming methods we expect to see.

8 April 1965

The telephone in the doctor's surgery, a taxi service, or even the grocery will always be answered – even when no one is in – now that the ansaphone has received Post Office sanction and become generally available in Britain. The machine, roughly the size of a portable gramophone, was developed by Southern Instruments (Communications) Ltd and, in common with most telephone equipment, is to be installed on a rental basis. The minimum cost of rental contracts including service and maintenance is £1 2s 0d a week.

22 January 1959

Telephone, radio, and television systems are capable of conveying information at a far greater rate than men and women can cope with it. This is shown by some recent measurements involving an application of 'information theory' to human beings. 'Information' in this technical sense includes all the entertainment and small change of ordinary conversation.

23 May 1957

NOTES

You can write your own questions (and answers!) here.